SOCIAL SKILLS FOR KIDS (AGES 5 TO 12)

13 STRATEGIES FOR BULLY BUSTING, FORGING UNBREAKABLE FRIENDSHIPS, PERCEIVING OTHERS' FEELINGS, AND RAISING SOCIALLY SMART KIDS

JOSH EVERMORE

© Copyright 2023 - **All rights reserved.**

The content contained within this book may not be reproduced, duplicated, or transmitted without direct written permission from the author or the publisher.

Under no circumstances will any blame or legal responsibility be held against the publisher, or author, for any damages, reparation, or monetary loss due to the information contained within this book, either directly or indirectly.

Legal Notice:

This book is copyright protected. It is only for personal use. You cannot amend, distribute, sell, use, quote or paraphrase any part, or the content within this book, without the consent of the author or publisher.

Disclaimer Notice:

Please note the information contained within this document is for educational and entertainment purposes only. All effort has been executed to present accurate, up to date, reliable, complete information. No warranties of any kind are declared or implied. Readers acknowledge that the author is not engaged in the rendering of legal, financial, medical or professional advice. The content within this book has been derived from various sources. Please consult a licensed professional before attempting any techniques outlined in this book.

By reading this document, the reader agrees that under no circumstances is the author responsible for any losses, direct or indirect, that are incurred as a result of the use of the information contained within this document, including, but not limited to, errors, omissions, or inaccuracies.

CONTENTS

Introduction   5

1. Leading the Way   11
2. Starting Strong (Ages 5 and 6)   25
3. Leveling Up (Ages 7 and 8)   71
4. Refining Social Skills (Ages 9 and 10)   121
5. Transitioning to Adolescence (Ages 11 and 12)   179

Conclusion   237
Acknowledgments   241
References   243

INTRODUCTION

We're losing social skills, those human interaction skills, how to read a person's mood, to read their body language, and how to be patient until the moment is right to make or press a point. Too much exclusive use of electronic information dehumanizes what is a very, very important part of community life and living together.

— VINCENT NICHOLS

We are currently flooded with technology. No matter where you turn, we're surrounded by tablets, phones, and laptops galore! One of the most pressing ways this affects us involves our kids. When we were growing up, our generations spent time playing outside and coming home before the streetlights filled the sky. Now, phones and tablets light things up instead. This has drastically impacted how kids—our future, as many say—connect, make friends, learn, and grow.

As parents or even educators of young minds, it's worrisome to think about how our kids can get the social skills they need to navigate daily life if they have their eyes planted on their screens at all times. While they may learn worthwhile things from the internet, genuine social interaction fails.

A familiar concern parents have—a question you may be asking—is what are our kids doing while they are in front of a screen? Are there unseen forces within the online world that may affect our kids negatively without us knowing, and how can we help with what we do not understand and cannot see for ourselves?

Just as in-person interactions can impact children's well-being, so can anything they see on the internet. Due to the privacy of technology, we see just part of the picture at all times. We struggle to know if our children are emotionally alright because the older they are, the more they shut us out of their screen time. Bullies are present all over the internet, and without the proper ability to control the internet itself—which is not a possibility for anyone—we do not know how to handle the frightening situations our kids may be getting into.

Given that internet terminology changes a lot faster than simple word of mouth—like the things you are more used to—the new words that your children are using could mean they feel good, bad, or otherwise without you knowing. And, scarily enough, you have no idea if the words they say relate to content that might not be age-appropriate. We have all heard specific acronyms and phrases that sound nonsensical to us but make perfect sense to our kids; sometimes, it's as if they are talking in verbal hieroglyphs.

You are not alone in the struggle. The first step is to admit the presence of the problem. This opens doors to helping your child that would have otherwise been unbeknown to you.

A great place to start is with my Social Superstar Strategies! You may wonder what these are. This is how you can assist your child in flawlessly prepping their social skills. After all, adults should always be positive role models for children and, as their parents, you're their first teacher. Teach your kid to be kind and patient since a child who sees such things will imitate them.

Role-play is another fantastic Social Superstar Strategy! Role-playing different everyday social situations with your child will give them good practice in interacting with real-life social problems—and it can even be a fun activity. Always, always, always teach your children empathy. When children have compassion, they will be more likely to respect and understand other people's troubles and feelings; compassion will also help them build an aptitude for charity, which is highly important for friendships and relationships.

Encourage listening—when a child learns to really listen to others, they will not subject themselves or others to meaningless conversations but communicate with rich meaning and understanding, furthering their social development. Always teach clear communication; without clarity, there is likely to be misunderstanding, resulting in social issues and other conflicts.

Be sure to always praise good behavior. Let the praise of a good deed accomplished by your child allow them to feel good so that they continue using positive behaviors. Please encourage your child to participate in group activities to get their socialization going. This can teach them essential values such as compromise, cooperating with others, teamwork, and friendship. Teach conflict resolution—you won't be sorry about doing this! When children learn how to solve conflicts strategically, lightheartedly, and peacefully, they are likely to maintain long-lasting friendships.

While you can't choose your children's friends, you can teach them how to pick the ones with healthy attitudes. When children learn how to make friends (and keep them), their self-esteem rises. Use active listening strategies and efficient verbal and nonverbal communication to help your kids achieve this!

Last but not least, you need to set expectations of appropriate behavior. Kids will absorb the environment, so setting proper expectations is very important. They must know there is a time and a place for acting in a certain way in a specific social situation. As the responsible adult here, it's your job to teach them how and why they must behave appropriately in various social situations.

If you've struggled with these contentious hurdles, you're in the right place; all the knowledge you need to get started is in front of you. Imagine that your child now always looks to you as a prime example of how they should behave, have many friends, and share what is going on in their life with you because they want to! Let's dive right into transforming the way your child socializes once and for all.

1

LEADING THE WAY

If a child lives with criticism, he learns to condemn.

If a child lives with hostility, he learns to fight.

If a child lives with ridicule, he learns to be shy.

If a child lives with shame, he learns to feel guilty.

If a child lives with tolerance, he learns to be patient.

If a child lives with encouragement, he learns confidence.

If a child lives with praise, he learns to appreciate.

If a child lives with fairness, he learns justice.

If a child lives with security, he learns to have faith.

If a child lives with approval, he learns to like himself.

If a child lives with acceptance and friendship, he learns to find love in the world.

— DOROTHY LAW NOLTE

LET'S TALK ABOUT SOCIAL SKILLS

We employ our social skills to communicate with others every day. Some commonly used examples are verbal and nonverbal skills, including specific body language and facial expressions. Children must understand these skills so they can have a fulfilling life.

It's amazing how learning social skills early on can impact a child's overall growth—even into adulthood. Children well-versed in social skills are more likely to achieve their high-school diploma and attend post-secondary education. They're also less likely to get into legal trouble or indulge in vices. Instead of taking up bad habits and hobbies, these kids will have better success at forming long-lasting friendships, developing their charisma, and becoming happier than children who are not socially versed.

As one Catholic Early EdCare (2021) article states, "Being active in the community, mixing with older people, and understanding what's happening in the local area all contribute to building social skills." Being part of a community gives a child a sense of belonging and a home away from their immediate home—and, of course, a way to learn from older people as well as gain many new friends who are in their community rather than just existing through a screen! Children who are not involved with their local communities are more likely to *not* find a connection with others who are around them. In this way, they end up with limited social bonds and an unconscious constraint against reaching out to people who "are not like me."

This is the central reason why people must have considerate social skills. The simple act of living in a community is marked by our emotions and engagement with others. These interactions are deeply interconnected. Comprehending our emotions forms the basis of our evolving mentality.

This mindset determines our decision-making process, which leads to our external responses. People see our actions but not the cogs and gears that churn behind them. With conscious and considerate thinking, we can show our children how sociability helps us reach out to others.

The Benefits of Social Skills

The direct benefits of efficient socializing and the skills needed for it are, in fact, visible from a young age.

A Better Quality of Life

In general, humans are a social species. We live and thrive better when we support each other. Community is apparent even to young children starting in peer groups. Take a kids' play area, for example. Some children make instant relationships after spinning around on the merry-go-round. In contrast, other children risk losing a possible connection because they are unwilling to share their swing even after staying on it for quite a while.

These social interactions can evolve or devolve based on the situation. The intensity of these moments is not lost on the children. They feel just as deeply as teenagers and adults when they are accepted into a friendship group—or rejected from it. By grasping keen socializing skills, the odds are on their side, and you'll witness kindergartners skipping around and forming strong bonds after sharing the seesaw! This, in turn, improves their connections with their new friend and ensures good experiences in the long run.

Everlasting Relationships

Socializing is a precursor to forming lifelong bonds. True compassion can be tough to fake. The more children experience genuine, morally good, and kind lessons about interacting with others, the better they get at weeding out people with ill intentions from their lives. Their circle of trusted loved ones will have strong characters, affirming each other without needing boosts of esteem from unscrupulous people.

Success at School

Schools are perhaps the first large social gathering most children attend regularly. As well as providing standardized education, school is a space of community and peer relationships that builds a child's personality over the years. You may notice that your kids are hesitant and nervous about starting a new grade. But when they make friends with their classmates, interact with their teacher and are treated well, they eagerly wake you up for school every morning, ready to begin the day! Similarly, it's crucial for homeschooled kids to find such friendships in other spaces in their lives.

Success at Later Stages of Life

Kids grow up aware of the world around them when they're capable of making these bonds. It's impossible to know everything in the universe, so the next best thing is to reach out to people who know more about a thing than you do. They may have friends who are great at specific hobbies and have excellent knowledge of their field. So, now, you know a guy who knows a guy!

You'll find many self-help books on how to forge partnerships and network through various companies. These books emphasize the importance of being able to connect with people who share a few interests with you (based on your college courses, research papers, or job prospects) or even zero interests. Properly done, the art of socializing will have you see these gaps not as barriers but as a leap over the hurdles just by being open and interested to learn!

When you teach your kids to harness these skills, tell them why they're important. Let them know that the traits of sharing and kindness are the fastest ways to gain friends, no matter where they go in life. It may be in a classroom, daycare, ballet class, fun house, or, really, anywhere!

THE PART YOU PLAY

Age-appropriate-social–emotional welfare is a key aspect of the social skills children are expected to use. This is possible based on what you teach them and how you do that. Lectures barely scratch the surface of true learning. Most kids imitate the behaviors around them. When they see the way you interact with known and unknown people, they mirror your stance, lexicon, expression, and tone. They recognize you as the blueprint of acceptable behavior in society. Even young kids are aware of wanting to fit in and be accepted by their community.

It's up to you to refine that hope for acceptance into good behavior and skilled socializing. They look up to you. Your job is to guide them through these lessons in gentle and respectful ways.

Take Albert Bandura's social learning theory, for instance. Though decades old, this theory carries worth since it demonstrates the importance of observation and social context when exhibiting behaviors. In 1961, a study of child participants observed adults being hostile toward a large Bobo doll. The group of kids who saw the grown-ups being verbally and physically aggressive toward the doll tended to mimic similar behavior to varying extents. The children who saw adults playing gently were less belligerent toward the doll.

The analyses of both groups were compared against a control group that did not witness either demonstration. The final results show that exposure to certain behaviors tended to coax children toward acting aggressively when placed in those exact situations (Bandura, 1977). These kids were young enough to not have the critical thinking skills that older children and teenagers develop thanks to healthy interactions with others.

Parental Support

Kids equate age with experience. Parents, older siblings, neighbors, and older friends take up a position of authority in a child's frame of reference. Our children rely on our judgment to formulate their first impressions. As they grow older, they learn how to develop these judgment-making skills. But, until then, most of their self-worth is directly influenced by us.

This is a huge responsibility. How do we administer level-headed and warm-hearted guidance to ensure they grow up with independence, clarity, and a healthy emotional mindset? It's one of the million relevant questions any new (or experienced) parent asks.

Support—not helicopter parenting, not ordering them around, and not leaving them to their devices all the time, but *genuine* support—and trust are crucial. It's popularly said that we don't just become brave or smart; we are thrust into situations that allow us to show bravery and intelligence.

When your kids are in a tough spot, what do you do:

- Do you leap in and show them the way out?
- Do you let them be and have them solve it on their own?

- Or do you stay with them and motivate their choices while letting them figure out the various parts of the situation to learn why one (or multiple answers) resolve the problem?

The third option builds the best character but is certainly not effortless.

Depending on the situation, you may respond differently. But if you assess that your child is not in immediate danger, you can let them think it over. Stay by their side and let them know they can ask you questions anytime. This is good practice for them to learn how to understand a situation, try various possibilities, and frame questions to help themselves. The more they ask, the better they get at asking.

So, even if you are not literally with them, your children will know how to deal with problems by taking the time to assess the issue and know when and how to ask for help. Recognizing their influence in any given situation is part of being socially aware. This is guaranteed by the vibrant and wholesome support of the nurturer.

Basic Skills

Listening

Strong communicators listen keenly. Young children are notorious for not having the patience to hear someone else's point of view. But, with repetition, you can nudge them toward the ethics of conversation. Let them know that everyone needs to be able to explain their perspective. This means when somebody is talking, your child should be able to exercise enough restraint to be able to listen to them instead of jumping into the middle of the conversation.

Inform them that the point of a conversation is to have everyone give their input. It doesn't mean the one who speaks the most or the loudest "wins." It means everyone can exchange ideas and come to a cohesive conclusion together.

Sharing

Though a fundamental lesson for all, not everyone is on board with sharing. Little ones have a hard time being separated from their beloved toys. A simple request to share contests their ownership of their things. Some children are wildly terrified we may take their stuff away. This is seen in the case of treats when we ask them to share a chocolate bar with their sibling.

The best way to prove the value of sharing is to show that they benefit from it as well. If you ask one child to share a crayon with a second kid, have the second kid loan something in return, like a pencil. This barter system works to an extent when all kids understand that they aren't "losing."

When children learn to share their stuff, they understand cooperation. Working with somebody in a group project, learning to play together by sharing a toy, and allowing others to take up space beside you are excellent examples of cooperation.

Following Directions

Instructing kids to follow certain rules is sometimes necessary, especially in the face of possible peril. There's no compromise to looking both ways before crossing the street. We may assume that kids understand the risk of disobeying rules, but that's not the truth. Always explain the reason. They ought to see you obeying these rules before they agree to them.

The level of inquisitiveness varies from child to child, but just wait, you'll be interrogated on why they need to use safety scissors while you get to use the shiny, pointy ones. Tell them the truth that practiced hands can handle the big kitchen scissors, while soft hands need to train with safety scissors for a few years. Take the time to explain the rules, and they will see the effort you put into maintaining them. This makes it easier for your kid to follow those rules as well.

Respecting Personal Space

This skill is about your kid understanding what personal space is, why it's important, and how to respect everyone's space. This goes both ways. Children must learn that their own space is valuable and that they will need to be able to say "no" to others encroaching upon their area. In the same vein, they must also avoid invading other people's spaces.

Young children often don't have the restraint to hold back from expressing enthusiasm. This is not inherently wrong, but as children reach the ages of four, five, and beyond, they recognize the value of showing excitement without impinging on another's space.

You can help them by showing how you reach out to others. Let them know that you can politely ask for handshakes or hugs before initiating them. Sometimes, the answer is "no." If you want them to understand the value of a refusal, you must do your best to agree with their rejections as well.

While it's hard to accept it when kids say "no" to green veggies, explain to them why veggies are good (they'll make you taller and stronger!) and then show them how you indulge in the delicacies of green, leafy vegetables. Repetition always helps. In this way, kids understand how powerful their expressions are and how everyone's words and physical space must be respected.

In the next chapter, you'll find out how children aged five and six put these basic skills to use and find their way into more complex social structures. This involves understanding the tools they have at their disposal and how to implement them in real-life situations.

2

STARTING STRONG (AGES 5 AND 6)

The path of development is a journey of discovery that is clear only in retrospect, and it's rarely a straight line.

— EILEEN KENNEDY-MOORE & MARK S. LOWENTHAL

From the age of five, kids begin to comprehend the foundational aspects of socializing in general. It's quite apparent if they've been exposed to a similar peer group at younger ages. This is when children transition from a self-centered mindset to recognizing others with different roles in their lives. Comprehending that the people around them have valuable input and their parts to play is a crucial step in building healthy relationships.

This chapter covers social development in the formative years of a child's life. The lessons they learn during this period will shape their personality for a lifetime. While it's possible to unlearn unhealthy characteristics, it is far more difficult to let go of them the older one gets. This is why we must cement ethical and healthy social habits from the get-go!

WHAT'S IT LIKE AT THIS AGE?

With great social skills comes great responsibility! As kids figure out how to tackle challenges using communication and cooperation skills, they grow more independent. You can help them value their agency by giving them simple chores such as cleaning up their toys after playtime or remembering to finish all their homework before dinner.

Careful integration of their chores into their daily routine builds a keen sense of duty. Congratulate them after they've finished their task before checking their work. If they've not managed it well, be overly positive and guide them as to the right way to do it instead of directly pointing out their faults.

A helpful article from the Centers for Disease Control and Prevention explores the kind of responses you can give to reduce unfavorable habits (2023):

Your child might start to "talk back" to feel independent and test what happens. Limit the attention you give to the negative words. Find alternative activities for her to do that allow her to take the lead and be independent. Make a point of noticing good behavior. "You stayed calm when I told you it's bedtime." (Tips and Activities section, para. 2)

As they grow, you can customize your responses based on their level of acceptance and confidence.

SOCIAL SUPERSTAR STRATEGIES

Here are 13 strategies that scaffold the lessons of ethical and social behavior for children aged five and six. The following chapters will revisit these strategies to show you how to build on them as your child grows older. We've touched upon some of them in the introduction to break the ice. Let's take a closer look at these tactics.

Strategy 1: Model Good Behavior

Researchers Alan Kazdin and Carlo Rotella rolled out the dire pitfalls of the infamous "do as I say, and not as I do" parenting style. In their words (2009):

The research points to three consequences of inconsistency. First, the effects of your teaching are diminished when deeds and words are not in line... Second, children can readily recognize inconsistencies, and they become more upset with their inconsistent parents than children who have more consistent parents... Third, a parent who does one thing but expects or demands the opposite from a child is more likely to have discipline problems and more likely to punish a lot to overcome the influence of his or her modeling. (para. 4)

As the parent or guardian, you are your child's first link to the world beyond. So, you are their premiere role model for good behavior.

Example: Your child and their friend are in the sandbox playing happily. You sit where the children can see you with the other kid's parent or guardian. You're sharing a plate of cookies you baked with that parent or guardian. The kids are intrigued and watch you and the other adult calmly take a couple of cookies each without bothering each other or making a fuss.

Let's use this simple scene to set the basis for how modeling good behavior allows your children to witness the benefits first-hand.

Polite Language

State your verbal requests or answers clearly and peacefully.

You: "Would you like a cookie?"

Other Parent (OP): "Yes, thank you!"

By keeping the conversation gentle with no raised voices, the kids observe that both parents receive a delicious treat without any arguments. Use pleasant words such as "please" and "thank you" in everyday interactions. Repetition is key, and kids always listen to how you talk to model their speech patterns.

Express Feelings Verbally

Be straightforward and state feelings, ideas, and intentions.

OP: "I would like to have another cookie. May I take it?" or "These are delicious! May I take one more?"

In the first case, the other parent expresses their wants. In the second, they compliment you and then express the want. If you demonstrate both scenarios to your children, you can show how being open about feelings can aid the situation and give the other parent a better shot of getting that cookie!

Demonstrate Empathy and Compassion

When possible, show that you are understanding of the other parent's (or participant's) situation.

You: "You can have the last one!"

OP: "Why, yes! Thank you so much!"

In this scene, you can have the other parent express gratitude for your offer. By offering the last treat, you show your kids that your wants may clash with another's wants, but showing compassion allows you to forge a strong bond with the other parent.

Practice Patience

Take the time to wait for a better reward later on.

OP: "I'll bring you some bagels tomorrow!"

You: "That sounds wonderful!"

This dialogue can follow the previous point where, since you surrendered the final cookie to the other parent, they choose to give you something in return. In essence, you're foregoing today's reward for tomorrow's gains. While this is not always true, you can still expose your kids to this scene to show that this is a possibility and that selfishness shouldn't stop them from helping out.

Resolve Conflicts Peacefully

Show a small dispute during the demonstration, which is then resolved neatly.

You: "You took five cookies and left me with just three?"

OP: "Oh, I didn't check."

You: "I wish I had gotten half of the plate."

OP: "I'm sorry. When I bring you the bagels, you can take an extra one!"

Conflict resolution will be discussed in detail in Strategy 8. The basics offered by this scene show how a sincere apology and an offer of more treats soothe the conflict. Sometimes, bringing in snacks seems like a precursor to bribes. You can rotate out the scene with any meaningful offer that both parties agree upon. But the apology is crucial!

What do the children gain from watching this polite interaction?

They observe patience and the potential rewards that follow respect. By sharing the cookies and resolving disputes, you and the other parent can maintain respect in your conversation, thereby strengthening your relationship.

Strategy 2: Role-Play

Role-playing is a nurturing approach where kids find freedom in their space of make-believe. As a caregiver or an educator, you can lay down the groundwork for the scene.

Sharing Toys

Set the stage. Sit with your kid with a few toys spread around you. Have them choose one and then jump in with a few compliments and descriptions of what you like about that toy. Engage in conversation with your child, expressing your interest and stating that you'd like to join in playing with the toy.

Measure their reluctance or interest and tweak your approach accordingly. The aim is to have them share the toy with you without too much complaint. For a first-timer, it can take a while, and that's fine! You can try this a couple of times with different toys and different people. Throughout the exercise, keep a cheery tone to encourage your child and reward them for their thoughtfulness.

Making New Friends

Reaching out to form new connections is certainly daunting, so your first step toward encouraging this is to try this make-believe game at home. Spin the tale of you and your kid hopping around an outdoor playground (it helps to skip about your house!) and coming across a neighborhood kid or someone from school.

Pose a question to your child about how they would approach the new kid. Let your child take the reins and describe the day. It's alright if they ramble on. Nudge them toward the topic and let them ponder over it. Maybe they can try the see-saw together or play tag around the playground. Whatever scenario they describe, congratulate them for being brave and inviting the new kid to play. Pick up the positive parts of the story and compliment them. Gently correct them on the negative aspects, if any.

Feeling Left Out

You can build on the previous scene for this one. Children generally don't like to be left out of fun activities. What will your child do if they see another kid in the playground, seemingly lonely and watching from afar?

Coach your kid on recognizing emotions of wonder and sadness in someone else's face. Let them decide whether or not to involve the third kid. If it takes them a while, you can ask point-blank how they would discuss with the second child, bringing the third one into their games. Communication and expression skills come into play here. Without knowing it, your child will be explaining their plans for socializing to you.

Recognizing and Handling Emotions

This make-believe game can deal with less-than-happy emotions, so let your child know that they can use as many words and take up as much space as they want. It helps them to know how free they can feel expressing difficult feelings.

Bring out the dolls and stuffed toys. Describe a scene to them where the dolls are playing hide-and-seek and cannot find one of the toys. You and your child will enact the dolls who are searching for their toy in vain.

Your child may talk about the dolls feeling dull, like a cloudy day, or having big, shouty emotions. You can ask your child to help the dolls and support them through the pain of losing the toy. They can even engage in a conversation with the dolls, explaining how it's okay to feel scared and worried before discussing places they can search for the toy. The aim here is for your child to express and validate the doll's feelings of fear and uncertainty, offer comfort, and help them.

Strategy 3: Teach Empathy

Five-year-olds can sense changes in emotions and expressions in their families and peers. They're becoming more intuitive about feelings because they start to make connections regarding shifting emotions.

This leads the way to empathy—understanding the depth of emotion in others since they've experienced similar situations. Try out these simple activities with your kid.

Understand and Describe

Various emotions bring a host of background information, given the context. When your child is in a good mood, ask them exactly how they feel. There can be a subtle difference between being happy and being excited. The best way for a child to understand individual feelings is to experience them. In this way, they can label each feeling, connect each feeling to the event, and gain a better comprehension of their mood in general.

For example, a child is happy that the sun is shining. But they are excited to go to the park. The more they explain and express their sentiments, the better they grasp the concept of similar but distinguishing emotions in others.

Stories and Shows That Explore Feelings

This can be a bedtime endeavor or a midday challenge. Sit with your kid and read a story or watch a show that focuses on feelings. Even in a tale of magic and adventures, the emotional journey of one of the characters is the connecting aspect to focus on. When you're done reading or watching, start a discussion with your child about their favorite character and how they think the character felt during the tale.

Books give kids a textual description of each character's journey and emotions, while TV shows and movies offer a visual story medium that displays emotions on the characters' faces. Both formats can teach children to decode external feelings and intentions.

Were there tough decisions the characters had to make about sharing their food or toys? Did you come across a sad or difficult moment when they had to pick themselves back up? Let your child describe the interesting points of the story and reflect on the character's choices. Praise them for figuring out what the character experienced throughout the story. The more they explain their feelings for the character, the better they'll understand similar instances in their peers and relatives. Recognizing emotional moments in others is part of their learning journey in empathy.

Discuss Pets and Their Feelings

This is a close-up of the previous activity in that the subject of your focus is right in front of your kid.

Growing up with a dog, a cat, or a bird adds to the experience of forming connections. If your child has no siblings, they will recognize their pet as the initial peer-like relationship before school and even neighborhood friends.

Observe how your child interacts with their pet. Do they scratch the cat gently? Do they feed the bird the right amount of treats? Do they pet the dog without too much force? Young kids may not have control over their enthusiasm, but by age five, they will learn how to tune their fine motor skills to offer gentler pats and rubs. Ask your child how the pet thinks about different people in the family. Start this conversation with the pet in the room, watch how your kid plays with them, and recognize the changing emotions in the animal's body language.

Strategy 4: Encourage Listening

We covered the importance of listening under the "Basic Skills" section in Chapter 1. Socializing and clear communication involves the task of listening keenly. Your child can earn the rewards of listening by paying close attention to instructions before the exercises below and within the games themselves. Here are some activities you can try with your kid if they're an only child or in a group of siblings, friends, or classmates.

Hot or Cold

Direct your kid to close their eyes and face away from you (or whoever it is). Hide a toy they are familiar with around the room or house. Now ask your child to search for it while listening to your clues. If they move closer to the hidden toy, call out, "Warm, hot, hotter!" If they move away, say, "Cool, cold, colder!" Their listening is essential to them finding the toy.

I Spy

This is a fun road trip game, but you can play it anywhere. Take turns describing a random object in your vision; for instance, "I spy with my little eye, a white fluff."

Your kid can scan around and point at clouds, marshmallows, or feathers if they're present around them. The objective is to allow your child to listen to your description and piece together your words to search for and find the object you're referring to.

Red Light, Green Light

You and your child stand at opposite sides of a room or open space. Announce, "Green light!" as you turn away from them. Your child should move toward you as quietly as possible. When you say, "Red light!" and spin back around, your child must freeze in place. If you see them move, you've caught them, and the game starts over.

This is a helpful exercise that allows kids to work on their listening skills and make quick decisions. Your instructions also reinforce the idea that red means stop and green means go, similar to traffic lights.

Copycat

You can stay seated for this activity. Face your child and say a random word. For simplicity's sake, go with popular words such as colors, fruits, vegetables, people's names, everyday objects, and the like. Your child repeats your word and adds another of their own to it. Then, you repeat the first and second words and add a third to it. Alternate your turns and keep adding words until one of you messes up the sequence or forgets the order of the words.

This game is based on pure listening skills and memory retention. The words are random and do not need to connect, thereby making it harder!

Guess Who?

You can play this without any tools or implements. A little similar to "I Spy," this game is about describing people in your life. Think of someone known to both you and your kid. With every turn, mention one facial feature or characteristic of this person. It can go like this: "The person I'm thinking of has glasses." Then your child guesses as to whom it might be. If they get it wrong, give them a second clue. With every wrong guess, keep encouraging them and give them another clue. The idea is to have your child hear the description staggered one element at a time and then piece those elements together to form a mental picture and win the game.

The above-mentioned games involve an element of play in the learning process. You can find more activities that pique your child's interest; some function well as single-person games, while others fare better with groups. When done well, these games help perfect your child's socializing by employing the skill of listening to people.

Strategy 5: Teach Clear Communication

Another developmental step is effective communication. Kids absorb information like a sponge, soaking up every word we utter and blabbering out anything they've learned. They have enthusiasm, and it's important to ensure we don't discourage them.

Avoid Poor Communication

Less-than-stellar and negative styles of conversation can lower self-esteem and create a toxic environment around your child. If an adult raises their voice and puts fury into their tone against a child, they impose their authority in a physical and psychological sense. The same is true if someone manipulates their words, gives their child 'the silent treatment,' always discourages them from questioning or exploring the world, constantly blames their kids for things beyond their control, and more.

Poor communication is not just about "describing" things incorrectly or conveying false feelings. When caring for a child, you must be aware of the power imbalance. A child is always dependent on their parent or guardian. They rely on the adult's perspective to gain confidence and dignity for themselves. Harmful communication can severely impact growth in their formative years. The most harmful varieties are abusive speech, passive-aggressive accusations, withholding truth, keeping secrets, blaming their kids' presence for any problems or issues that occur, outright threatening them, and even neglecting the child altogether.

Good communication, in general, has a positive influence on a child's emotions and words, while poor communication invalidates them. This is how language skills develop. It's important to give children opportunities to talk about their thoughts and ideas. Exercises like storytelling, group discussions, and active listening nurture their ability to speak clearly and with confidence.

Show-and-Tell

In the classroom, "Show-and-Tell" is a popular game that shines the spotlight on children talking about their favorite things. The benefit is twofold in that the activity allows everyone to understand the importance of the object or hobby your child is eager about, and your kid gets the chance to express their enthusiasm and feelings about the topic. It's an incredibly simple and effective exercise in teaching your child to articulate their thoughts.

Puppet Play

This is a scenario where you give your child a soft toy puppet that they can maneuver with their hand. The puppet should have vibrant facial features with exaggerated eye and mouth placement. Caregivers have noted an increased response in communication when a child uses a puppet to talk about their feelings as though in the third person (Elder, 2020).

Here's what one children's organization has documented about this kind of communication (MVP Kids, n.d.):

Puppet use increases a child's interest in practicing social skills, allowing caregivers to repeatedly target a child's needs in a fun and engaging way... Allow reluctant communicators to use a puppet to discuss emotions and process feelings, challenges, or traumas they might have experienced. (para. 8)

Strategy 6: Praise Good Behavior

The positive, happy route is the best option to take. It is important to catch instances of good behavior to encourage it in your child. Kids thrive off of optimistic feedback and often do good solely to achieve their parents' praise. It's important to note that positive reinforcement at a young age will instill the duty of being polite and good when your child is older. Though they expect rewards now, this will diminish, and their self-esteem will be strong enough to not need recompense for every good deed.

We must give praise that is proportional to the action. Avoid negative reinforcement, even if it is intended to discourage unhealthy behaviors. This only enforces the idea that adults are willing to resort to unsupportive language and actions, and it instigates the child to try such behavior as well.

It's also vital to avoid being overly cheerful for smaller duties. If a child refrains from yelling during a time, they must be quiet (such as nap time), congratulate them lightly, and help them move on to another task. If they help with chores or tasks that are not usually within their purview, that invites greater praise because it wasn't expected from them in the first place. You'll find your rhythm as you practice this daily. Here are some examples.

Politeness

"You said 'please' and 'thank you' at lunch today. That's very polite!"

Recognizing small examples of good behavior shows your child that you're an active part of their life and that you appreciate their polite and kind words or acts.

Try New Things

"I noticed you tried the peas at dinner, even though you were unsure. I'm proud of you for trying new things."

At varying levels, it's hard to try new things for fear of failing. Being congratulated for taking up a new task or hobby can instill greater confidence in the long run.

Effort

"Wow, you tried so many times to tie your shoes, and you didn't give up. That's a great effort!"

With appropriate validation, children will be emboldened to do their best at various tasks. They will focus on the attempts and their effort to do the right thing rather than worrying about failure.

Cleaning Up

"I love how you picked up all your toys without being asked. That's a big help!"

Chores are a unique part of character building. Proper praise will motivate your child to pick up after themselves as a daily routine.

Listening (Patience)

"You did a great job of listening to the story today! You were quiet and patient."

Many skills are interconnected, and mastering one helps develop the other. When a child learns to be patient, they can foster better conduct and listen to people without interrupting them.

Strategy 7: Encourage Group Activities

Healthy peer relationships inspire a child's esteem and reduce inner conflict. Well-conducted group activities are a surefire way to enhance social skills and development for kids of all ages. This is seen in an advertisement about Team Big Ben Kids' work with children's group exercises (I Am Expat, 2021):

Even at a young age, creative activities help develop creative thinking and basic mathematical skills, such as geometry (size and shape), measuring, and sorting. There is also a great deal of problem-solving and concentration that happens when children learn to express themselves or put what they have in their heads on paper. (para. 2)

You can conduct several age-appropriate activities with the range of toys and tools that you have available. State your instructions clearly. You may have to repeat them for the rules to sink in.

Scribble Drawing

Similar to "Copycat," this is a drawing game. Divide the kids into a couple of teams with a reasonable number of children in each one. Give each team a sheet of paper and a pencil. Let the first child in each team draw a random scribble. The second child adds their doodle. So does the third, and then the fourth, and so on. The team that ends up with a drawing that looks most like an actual image wins!

Lego Building Challenge

This requires Lego building blocks or any kind of blocks that can form colorful structures. You, the judge, assign a minimum of three kids per team. Each kid will have a role. One is a looker or an observer. The judge provides them with a picture of a finished Lego structure; it can be as simple or as complex as you want. The second kid is the messenger. Messengers are mobile. They run between the first and the third team members. The observer explains to the messenger how the Lego structure looks using shapes, colors, and numbers to describe it.

The messenger rushes to the third kid, the builder, and describes to them how the structure should look. The builder assembles the model with the pieces they have. The team whose structure is the closest to how the judge's picture looks wins the game!

Fill the Bucket

Now we're outdoors! Divide the kids into teams. The greater the number of kids, the more fun! Give each team an empty bucket. Their objective is to fill the bucket with water before the other team does. Each player must use their hands to transfer the water from the source (a tub or a tap) to their bucket.

Team Scavenger Hunt

Similar to "I Spy," this involves groups of children challenging each other to complete the game. Build a list of items and write them down on a board or a sheet of paper. To make it simpler, attach a picture of the object beside the name. These items must be hidden around the room or in a contained area if you're outdoors. Give the kids a time limit. The team that finds the most objects wins the game!

Collaboration is key. The teams that cooperate and communicate well will have the advantage.

Strategy 8: Teach Conflict Resolution

As with any group of people (no matter their age), friction can arise. Some kids are unwilling to share their stuff, and some are hesitant to involve children other than their friends in games. You can introduce them to conflict-resolution strategies to help them be open with their feelings and learn how to understand different viewpoints. As explained in the previous chapter, cooperation is a boon, and using this prowess in playtime enhances the quality of social gatherings.

The idea behind incorporating conflict-resolution strategies is to ensure every child gets a chance to speak up and be heard. During a disagreement, a group of children can utilize these skills to be patient and listen to everyone's suggestions. Thus, the resolution of a challenge is tackled by the entire group and not just by the loudest kid (Anderson College, 2015).

Imagine the class hamster has run away from its cage. Try the below techniques to familiarize kids with how to handle the situation gently and respectfully.

Calm Down

When encountering a problem, kids may freeze or immediately rush to an adult. But you can set a safe space for the children to take their time and become acclimatized to the idea of staying calm during the issue. Inform them they have ample time. Let them use this given time to avoid shouting and instead ensure everyone is alright. The objective is for them to know that you care for them and for every kid to reach out to each other and make sure no one is debilitatingly worried about the missing hamster. And if someone is distressed, the first order is to help calm them down.

Figure Out What's Wrong

Start the discussion. If your children or students are shy, you can get the ball rolling by mentioning a few things about the hamster. Get the kids talking about the missing rodent and its favorite things to do or spots to visit around the house or classroom.

Encourage Listening

When one child talks, the others must stay quiet and listen. You can set the example by staying still and giving each child your full attention. If anyone interrupts them, gently remind them to let the first kid finish speaking.

Also, make sure that the kids don't go too off-topic. Some may begin to ramble and derail the conversation. Remind them of what's at stake and steer them back to the situation at hand.

Show Compassion

It's possible one of the kids may have accidentally left the hamster cage unlocked or may not have shut it properly. But the group must stay calm and not outright accuse that kid of being careless. You may have to intervene if voices are raised, but you can make a preliminary statement, saying, "Now we know Sandra was the last one to feed our little hamster. But let's not point fingers. It could have happened to any of us. She was brave to tell us that she saw him last. Let's go from there and see what could have happened."

When you show consistent empathy toward the children, they will respond in kind.

Find Solutions Together

After every child has spoken up, let them come up with suggestions. They may have opinions on different possibilities, and these need to be heard as well. Ask them to use their words to explain why certain recommendations may not work or why they would.

"I think Max's idea to search the playground is not helpful because the hamster is probably inside the house/classroom."

"Darla's idea of checking the cubbies is great! The hamster likes to sleep in the afternoon, so he might have gone there."

Articulating thoughts is a tough and learned skill. These are the situations where kids must use their growing vocabulary to explain their ideas and intentions in well-meaning ways.

Strategy 9: Guide Them in Making Friends

Friends: The Greatest of All Time

As mentioned in Chapter 1, we gain a better quality of life by forming strong and dependable social connections. In the long run, various kinds of partnerships can form and fail over time, but family and friends are perhaps the best and longest-running relationships that can be worked on. No matter how young a child is, they can grasp the strength of a valuable peer in their life. We must help them build the skills to be able to choose the right people and form healthy bonds.

We need not aim at transforming every kid into a vibrant social butterfly. Not everyone is an extrovert. But it's possible and recommended that we encourage all children to socialize and strive for the confidence they need to reach out to friends (Bayless, 2022).

Approach With a Friendly Greeting

This helps in a classroom setting. The first day of school is nerve-wracking enough, given that kids have to spend hours away from their families. Making friends is a tall hurdle to get over, but once that's successfully done, the school can become a beloved place.

You can motivate your child to find one other kid in the room and strike up a conversation with them. A cheerful or polite "Hey" or "Hi" can commence a bubbly little conversation between the two kids.

Say Their Name

Some schools may have each kid's name printed on a tag on their shirt or on their coat hooks, cubby holes, or tables. If some children find it difficult to read the names, or if these tags are not available, asking each other for their names is also a great conversation starter. A name is an integral part of a person's identity, so giving each other their due regard by calling them by their name is a wonderful way to break the ice.

Listen and Respond

Keep an eye on the kids, who seem rather quiet. Perhaps the conversation has fizzled out. You can motivate them to ask questions and find out more about each other. This involves keenly listening to a fellow child's response and pursuing more about their answer.

"I have lots of pink scrunchies at home."

"Wow! I like pink. Is that your favorite color?"

"Yes! My lunch box is also pink! What's your favorite color?"

It may take a while, but when kids learn how to jump from one topic to another, there's no end in sight!

Common Interests

Have the kids discuss a topic that they share an interest in. It can be anything from their favorite flower to the best cookie they've ever had. When kids find something that helps them connect, they can jump from topic to topic in a stream of consciousness. Sometimes, all you have to do is nudge them toward that starting field of interest!

Ask Open-Ended Questions

Another way of getting a conversation going is by asking children an imaginative question. Their creative juices will start flowing, and they will have diverse responses to the question.

"What shape is that cloud over there?"

"What's your favorite dinosaur?"

The conversation that sparks from this is generally filled with delight and learning, especially since such questions need not have a solid numerical or yes or no answer.

Play Together

Try pairing the children up. This way, you start small. Give a single toy to each pair of kids and encourage them to start a conversation about it. If the toy is a train engine, the children can make up a story of being conductors on a train, traveling around the countryside. The exercise of talking out loud helps develop their language skills and their emotional expressions of excitement and happiness. The act of sharing is its virtue, and the kids will be able to get along better with the aid of the story they make together.

Strategy 10: Discuss Nonverbal Communication

Conveying messages without speaking is more than staying quiet and sending written notes. Even young children recognize certain subtle messages given to them in a social space.

- **Body movement:** A child notices when someone presents nervous, confident, happy, or sad body language. Fidgeting in their place, breathing heavily, laughing loudly, and hunching their shoulders are movements that convey significant emotion.
- **Touch:** The way someone reaches out to hold your hand and the feelings you get from skin contact can give varying indications. Discussing good touch and bad touch and what to do when the situation is not optimal becomes vital.
- **Eye contact:** You can portray emotion in your eyes by squinting and widening them. Humans can recognize the shape of the face even as newborns. They understand that the eyes are the place to see. Visually strong kids instantly understand the weight of emotion behind someone's gaze.
- **Facial expression:** These range from the simplest expressions of smiles and frowns to complex ones of fear, grief, enthusiasm, and

more. Our eyes crinkle, our eyebrows scrunch and separate, the shape of our mouth turns up or down, and our skin wrinkles, all of which convey expressions and meaning.
- **Space:** Personal space speaks volumes. Some have little to no need for personal space and are eager to initiate contact in the form of hugs, handshakes, and more. Others need a safe bubble around them. It's often easy to perceive how people are by the way they acknowledge and respect others' personal space.

With effective empathy, kids engage better with their peers without the need for spoken words. Here are some activities you can conduct to help them comprehend meaning and messages without speaking.

Emotion Charades

Just like regular Charades, the kids will need to act out the word. In this version, you'll write down the names of emotions on pieces of paper for each child to read. One by one, they'll then use facial expressions and body movements to express their emotion to their friends or classmates. Their demonstration must not use words, but they can be as creative as possible to show large movements or subtle expressions.

Expressive Storytelling

This can work with a group or one on one with your child or student. Read out a fun storybook and inject as much energy as you can by voicing different characters uniquely based on the emotional tone of the story. Embellish the character tones and the story plot in creative ways.

When you're done, start a discussion with your child to get them to recount the story similarly. They may use the same tactics you did to exaggerate the characters' voices, or they may add their twist to the presentation.

Point out how the story seems different thanks to the diverse ways you and the kid voiced the story. Emphasize the strength of emotion and how it elevated the experience.

The Mirror Game

This is a pretty simple and fun game you can try with very young kids. Stand in front of a mirror so your child can see you and themselves as well. In the first round, you will show an exaggerated version of common emotions: happy, sad, or mad. Have your kid copy your facial expressions before asking them to name the emotions. Once they understand what these feelings mean, you can increase the difficulty in the next round using these emotions: scared, worried, and excited.

Observing these emotions on their face familiarizes your kid with their body language and expressions. In this way, they'll know how to convey these feelings to others without the need for words if the situation demands it.

Strategy 11: Teach Patience

The Manthan School is an organization that values teaching younglings lessons in patience (2023):

Patience is a virtue that is essential for children to learn. It helps them to cope with difficult situations, understand other people's points of view, and to control their own emotions and impulses. When children are patient, they are more likely to succeed in school and social relationships. (para. 15)

This organization recognizes the importance of patience and how learning about it at a young age ensures kids have a stable grasp on socializing as they grow. You can make these lessons fun by using the following tips to engage with kids:

- **Get on their level:** Sit down with them and have a frank conversation about the things that are at the forefront of their mind. It may be

about things you would never have given a second thought. For example, your child may prefer orange juice over milk, and it frustrates them to drink milk every morning. By keeping eye contact with them and giving them your full attention, you're letting them know that their concerns are important to you as well.
- **Offer choices:** You can brainstorm with them on possibilities. Maybe breakfast will include OJ on alternate days or the weekends. That way, your child has milk semi-regularly while also getting to indulge in their favorite drink. Involving them in the situation gives your child more agency over these decisions.
- **Encourage participation:** You can include your child even more by bringing them into breakfast decisions: "What shall we have tomorrow?" and "How about something healthy on Tuesday and something fun on Wednesday?" Holding these discussions can teach them the value of being able to hear you patiently and offer their suggestions in return.

Fun activities based on waiting are abundant. Kids can try these out on their own or in groups!

Story Circle

Assign kids space to sit in a circle facing each other. They should each be holding a beloved toy at this point. Give them directions to explain the importance of their toy from the toy's perspective. For example, your child might talk about their teddy bear being a brave knight who fights off shadows at night.

Whatever the story, all the children are to take turns and listen to each other. This teaches them patience, listening, and impulse control. If they can stop themselves from interrupting another child, it means they're truly immersed in the story and can connect with their peers in the experience of it.

Gardening

This is a tough one, but it gives incredibly fruitful results when done well! Procure a garden pot and healthy seeds (marigolds, sunflowers, zinnias, or other fast-growing plants). Follow the instructions based on the seeds you've chosen. Supervise your child as they dig a hole in the soil, plant the seeds, and water the pot as needed.

Help keep up their enthusiasm by observing when the leaves, flowers, and fruits sprout. The longer they keep at it, the better their patience will be rewarded with a healthy plant.

Strategy 12: Teach Respect

Respect can, unfortunately, be misinterpreted as a loaded word that's a substitute for obedience and blind faith. But true respect means acknowledging everyone's space and dignity no matter the situation. If you can guide your kids to listen and care about their peers, family, and themselves, they will have mastered the most complex of social skills.

You can respect the opinion of people you do not agree with by understanding that everyone deserves to be heard. But it's also important to learn to stand up for yourself and develop self-focused courtesy.

Understanding respect involves patience and listening to other people. Kids who can pay attention to their classmates gain a better understanding of how valuable different perspectives are. You can try these games to help children practice respecting people's suggestions, opinions, belongings, and personal space.

Role-Playing

This game focuses on asking permission before borrowing a friend's belongings. You can demonstrate this and give the kids examples of how to ask politely:

"I can't find my pencil, and I need to finish my homework! May I borrow yours for a while?"

"This cookie looks delicious. May I have a piece?"

Direct the conversations and questions so that the kids recognize the value of the item they're borrowing, whether they can return it or if it's a snack or juice box for them to consume. Switch the children around so they are also on the other end, hearing the request and deciding to part with their beloved belongings.

Pillow Tosses

This works with a group of kids or with a single child and you. Obtain a toy, such as a light ball or pillow, that young children can easily throw and catch. Set the rule that the person holding the pillow is the only one allowed to talk at that moment. You can choose a topic that the kids are interested in, or you can have them select a category, such as their favorite toy, color, or snack.

Kids can pass the pillow around in a circle or toss it to anyone they desire (it'll be up to you to ensure everyone gets a chance to speak). Whoever is holding the pillow has the chance to announce their likes and dislikes regarding the topic, and everybody else must listen. If anyone disagrees, the pillow can be tossed to them, and they can politely state their preferences without accusing the previous child of "bad" opinions or tastes.

Offering respect is part of the journey of developing empathy and compassion. This is a time-taking endeavor, and you'll see your child will take a while to move away from a self-centric worldview to a more integrated one that involves the presence of others around them.

Strategy 13: Set Expectations

Kids need to have clear expectations of their environment, the people around them, and their behaviors.

With skills of patience, communication, and respect, children are better able to share, collaborate, and even brainstorm and problem-solve through difficult situations without adult interference. Working on such crucial social journeys in the incredibly low-risk space of play helps develop vital life skills with less worry or trauma.

It is not easy to root substantial expectations within young children. How do you tell your kids how much is too much or what lines to simply not cross? It's about developing independence along with responsibility in their character. Your kids must have the confidence to venture into the world and build relationships, but they must also have respect and patience for others' perspectives and cultures. Your children ought to show kindness and be grateful to their trusted loved ones, but they also must not allow others to walk on them by people with unhealthy intentions.

It's a daunting tightrope to cross. You can work off of these three routes to figure out how to develop your solutions.

Connect With Their Age

It's not easy being a child while also being aware of the adult world. At a certain age, kids know that adults rule the world. Adults create the laws and wield consequences if rules are broken. When kids can discern the power their parents, guardians, teachers, and others hold over them, it's up to us to ensure that our authority is not a chokehold on their freedom and development but is instead a foothold.

You must guide and nurture your child using your experiences and power to keep them as safe as possible while they grasp the knowledge and skills needed at every milestone. Understand that their age isn't a barrier but the answer to how to bond with them.

Be Patient About the Big Picture

As mentioned in Strategy 11 about teaching patience to young ones, it takes time for children to become acclimatized to not receiving instant gratification. In the same way, you must be ready to wait things out because expectations are meant to fuel long-term gains. Your children's goals are not meant to be just for the current week or month. Major behavior settings that deal with socializing skills must last a lifetime.

Life constantly shifts gears without telling us in advance, so you must be as prepared as possible. It's alright to feel curious and worried but do not let this stop you from fortifying your kids' future by emboldening them today.

Recognize When It Is and Is Not Working

Certain strategies are not suited to all. You must tailor your approach based on how your child responds to various environments and stimuli. For example, neurodivergent children will need a different format of attention than that preferred by neurotypical kids. Your work becomes easier when you accept that some methods will hinder your child's progress. It means you'll start searching for the right ways faster.

This realization can happen on its own, but it's best aided by a teacher who capitalizes on your child's empathy by using various strategies to guide them. Children are a product of their upbringing, culture, race, gender expression, and so many more categories that are visible only when we accept our kids unconditionally. It's all about how safe and free we make them feel.

Parents and teachers can open discussions on emotions and tell stories where a character has relatable feelings that a child can easily pick up and comprehend. In this way, your kid can be open about their feelings without feeling the need to bottle things up. They can also recognize and validate feelings in others, which builds into sympathy—relating to the feeling but not the experience necessarily—and compassion—showing kindness even when they don't understand the experience.

When you accept natural limitations and customize your nurturing to your child's needs, they'll follow your example and be just as open and accepting of their friends and family.

The best part of figuring out these strategies is that kids are constantly learning how to be better versions of themselves. It's already within them. They simply have to uncover it. Know that the 13 strategies listed in this chapter adapt to kids as they grow. I've also created a section in each chapter entirely for your kids. Let them read through the information below and pick up their own ideas!

KIDS' CORNER

Did you know a good way to make friends is to give them your name? You can find out a lot about your siblings, cousins, classmates, and neighbors by figuring out how to talk to them.

I told the grown-ups how to help you make friends wherever you go, but here's a special message just for you! You'll get a lot of chances to find people who are also searching for friends. And the best part is, they're probably searching for you too.

Here are some ideas you can use to get started.

- You can introduce yourself by telling them about your name like this:

    "Hi, my name is _____. What's yours?"

- Can you tell if someone looks sad? Maybe their eyes are all watery, or they have a runny nose. Next time you see someone unhappy, try telling them a joke. That might cheer them up.

    "What's a bear with no teeth? A gummy bear!"
    "How does a bee reach school? On a school buzz!"

- Some kids are pretty quiet. See if they're okay with you sitting next to them. You can ask them to play a game with you if it's playtime at school. Sometimes, they won't want to play with anyone! That's okay. Remember, don't bother them. You can do that if they don't mind you sitting with them. Then neither of you will be alone!
- Find a grown-up that you know is okay to get some advice. It's not easy to make friends, trust me! If you need help, ask for it! Everyone needs someone. Some days you need someone to hold your hand and tell you you're doing great. Today, it's me! You're doing a fantastic job, kiddo!

In the next chapter, we'll see how our Social Superstar Strategies evolve to suit children aged seven and eight. Time never stops, and neither do we. Let's get crackin'!

3

LEVELING UP (AGES 7 AND 8)

You have brains in your head. You have feet in your shoes. You can steer yourself in any direction you choose.

— DR. SEUSS

Children entering the second grade are in the throes of social development and emotional engagement. They're aged seven to eight years, and our focus as parents, caregivers, or educators is on their grasp of utilizing the foundational aspects of social behavior in life.

By now, we can assume your child is set in a daily routine and has a healthy outlook on emotional understanding and connecting with the world. Let's learn how to cultivate more specific techniques within this stage of their growth.

WHAT'S IT LIKE AT THIS AGE?

Seven- and eight-year-olds can branch out and connect with their peers—or, at least, have the desire to do so. They're inclined to form partnerships with other kids of the same gender. Their social demands are less self-centered and more about group connections. Kids at this age will be more inclined to form their identity around their relationships with their peers and family. To them, the rite of being accepted into their peer community is one of the more important wants to be fulfilled.

With this healthy understanding, they will likely support each other within the team and may even trash-talk opponents! But, of course, that is learned behavior. If your kids observe positive or negative responses and actions from their peers, they will imbibe those similar traits.

Since children develop and socialize at their own pace, the generalized guidelines may not always match your kid's experience. So, proceed with an open mind and a grateful heart, and don't lose faith if you fear that they are falling short of milestones. They're still blossoming.

SOCIAL SUPERSTAR STRATEGIES

Here, we're circling back to the 13 tactics discussed in Chapter 2, which have now evolved to aid seven- and eight-year-olds in their social world.

Strategy 1: Model Good Behavior

The more company kids keep, the more their observational skills grow. There's a keen difference between children from stagnant environments and those with diverse social backgrounds. For example, an only child will have a candid and open rapport with their parents, while a set of siblings will tend to be more boisterous than when they're with their folks.

Neither of these settings means that the child is better or worse off. It just indicates how the environment and the people in it influence their social education.

Positive Interaction

Introduce complex behaviors. Stay quiet when somebody explains a subject you might not be familiar with. Your children will take in your attentive body language and interested facial expressions and incorporate those actions into their character. Kids are very impressionable, so you have to uphold healthy activities as much as possible.

Model long-standing empathic habits such as offering help, recognizing emotions in others, and more. Browse through the following strategies and see how many of them you can add to your daily interactions. The more consistently you demonstrate healthy interactions, the better your child will adapt to similar behaviors.

Conflict Resolution

We'll cover how to teach conflict resolution to kids in Strategy 8. But when you illustrate the right ways to confront a problematic situation, it becomes a learning moment for your child.

Approach your difficult situation with a clear head. Show confidence and a willingness to learn. Your child shall require effective communication and patience. You and a partner can demonstrate how you'd resolve a problem with your child. Perhaps your partner lost your pen or messed up a stacked house of cards. These scenarios show that while fixing the problem is complex, you can still figure out a decent solution without losing your cool.

Continue Empathy and Compassion

Your child ought to be consistent with their empathetic behavior throughout life. Thus, you'll find the best results if you imbibe these skills on a long-term basis.

This is a continuing message from Chapter 2. Exemplify the virtue of showing compassion and being kind to each other, and your kids will follow your lead.

They see you. They notice how you behave with others and how you treat the people around you. In the wise words of the quirky movie *Ant-Man*, "You're her hero, Scott. Just be the person she already thinks you are" (Reed, 2015, 17:26).

Respect Diversity

Integrate broader ideas to help familiarize kids with inclusive language that does not discriminate or separate anyone. This consideration for diversity is vital to today's world, where the population is teeming with people of varying cultures, races, genders, orientations, and more.

For example, it's not dignified to point at someone in a wheelchair and loudly ask intrusive questions. You can instead mention, "Yes, that person needs to use a wheelchair to get around. If you want to ask, you must be polite and nice. And if they don't want to talk about it, just wish them a good day!"

Emphasize treating everyone with different experiences fairly. It helps children build strong ideas about the world. Kindness becomes a grounding feature in our empathetic connections.

Strategy 2: Role-Play

Role-playing helps a child channel heavy emotions indirectly. Here are four tough cases that they can face in reality. Stress the concept of acting out roles to let kids understand the pain and power of being in these situations.

Peer Pressure

Scene: Keep an apple on the teacher's desk. Have one student tell the other to eat the apple. The second child must refuse.

"No, that's the teacher's apple! We shouldn't take it."

"The teacher will be mad if we eat their apple. Let's do something else."

"Maybe we can ask the teacher for the apple? They might share it."

The children can assert themselves in various creative ways. Emphasize how the apple is dear to the teacher, who will be sad, worried, or annoyed about losing it. By bringing up emotions, kids can better understand the consequences. Praise them for their acting to cement your approval of their choice to not take the apple.

Dealing with Disappointment

Scene: It's Show-and-Tell season! Show one student winning the game and a second child feeling sad and annoyed.

"I did my best and had fun. That's good."

"I know where I went wrong. I'll be better in the next game!"

"My friend won because they spoke really well. I'm proud of them."

Everyone encounters failure at some point in their life. You can show how this isn't always a bad thing but simply a short-term setback. People learn during rejections and failures. Even though kids feel disappointed, it's not the end of their lesson but the beginning of another. Validate the child's feelings before congratulating them for their good attitude.

Handling Teasing

Scene: One child is being teased by another (or a group) about their new haircut. Have the student stand up for themselves.

"I like my hair. It's really nice!"

"You don't need to be mean about my hair."

"I spent the whole day out with my Dad, and we got ice cream after my haircut!"

The kids can be staunchly assertive or overly positive in their responses. It's important to coach them against escalating the situation. Rotate the groups so that the kids who acted out the teasing also get to play the role of someone being teased. Some situations can vary, with the kids having to stand their ground and respond "no" to the teasers.

Strategy 3: Teach Empathy

It's easier to empathize with people who are similar to you than with those who have greater differences. But that shouldn't stop you from extending a helping hand. Coach your children and students to understand the reality and substance of their experiences.

Pet Care

Grasping the nuances of an animal's emotions is a grand adventure for the growing child. They get to learn firsthand that pets have specific likes and dislikes. Some animals like extended belly rubs, and others skitter away from prolonged contact.

Observe your child's interaction with the pet before guiding them. What does your pet like in the way of emotional or mental stimulation? Some dogs love strictly outdoor games, some cats love music, and some birds love delightful little puzzles. Most of them need baths and proper grooming too. Involve your child or student in these activities, and the pet will soon recognize that playtime involves this young human as well! You can form a schedule and let your child lead the activity. Kids do well with routines, and some animals adore them as well!

Kindness Challenge

Set a small challenge with a deadline, before which the kid must do something good for another person without the expectation of a reward. Praise them for their efforts every time they figure out how to help others.

This can be tough, so work up to it. The first week can have them helping you or a sibling with small chores. They can get a small bonus on their allowance or extra time before curfew. In the second week, they might share toys with a friend without being asked. You can give them tangible rewards on alternate weeks. Start a discussion of how they felt while helping others. Focus on how their emotional gratification is a valid form of empowerment.

Embrace Diversity

Invite Everyone to Play

Touching upon the aspect of recognizing and accepting diversity from Strategy 1, you can set up simple games and activities that guide kids to involve each other and make sure no one is left behind. Encourage cohesive playtime between girls and boys. Have the more outgoing students invite the more socially awkward ones. Their enthusiasm can be contagious!

Sharing Games

Some children may bring a lot more stuff (toys, pencils, colors) to school than others. You can mention the disparity gently and encourage more sharing across the board. This includes experience too! For example, a child who needs to use crutches may suggest games that involve less physical activity and more mental stimulation. They can introduce new board games and puzzles and bring their unique energy to each different game.

Celebrating Differences

Kids discover that they've honed their talents in different areas. Some may be adept at addition, some are better at drawing, while others can spell the best. Students can be grouped into teams, each team containing kids specialized in certain subjects. They can help each other with their homework, studies, games, and more. That way, everyone gets to shine, with equal time and attention given to all.

Healthy Limits and Boundaries

Bodily autonomy and decision-making power are not often within a child's ability. The world—with all its terrible truths—is not built for innocence. It's up to you to empower kids with the tools they need to state their boundaries. All "nos" are "hard nos." Consent is not just to do with adult activities but also with the approval of skin contact.

Children have the biggest say over their bodies. If they do not wish to hug someone, you and the other kids (and adults) must respect that decision. Beyond touch sensitivity and stimming (a semiconscious physical or vocal stimulation, such as hand waving or humming, aimed at reducing overwhelming sensations), some kids simply need pure trust to know that they are validated. When you ask their permission to shake hands, embrace them, pick them up, and so on, you are proving the worth of their space. In this way, they are also encouraged to respect the bodies of other children in all situations.

Strategy 4: Encourage Listening

Active listening is the foothold of any good conversation. By the ages of seven and eight, kids generally are able to hold effective conversations by stating their piece and then staying quiet to hear out other people. But are they passively receiving counterarguments, or are they genuinely listening?

Encourage children to be fully involved in the dialogue even when they're not talking. You can coach them to hold eye contact for a few consecutive seconds, at least. Eyes are a strong fixture. Some people cannot maintain steady eye contact for long or at all. To overcome any awkwardness, you can guide your kid to fix their gaze at the bridge of the speaker's nose or near their eyebrows. This way, they show clear interest in the other person's words.

Being able to respond to what they've heard is a great skill. You can help kids build questions or answers to anything the other party mentions. Here's an example.

Kid 1: "My sunflower grew two feet tall. I'm waiting for the full flower."

Kid 2: "That's awesome! My sister's sunflower has already bloomed. I can ask her how long she waited."

Kid 1: "Yeah, thanks!"

This format of response builds off of what the speaker has said. It shows a genuine ebb and flow of conversation rather than two kids speaking out loud on disconnected topics.

Listening Games

Simon Says

This is best played with a group, but you and your kid can make it fun as a pair as well. Stand facing your kid and give physical movement instructions, some of which should begin with "Simon says…"

For example, "Simon says, hop on one leg and laugh."

If you include "Simon says" before the instruction, your child must perform the motion. If you do not say the titular words, your child must remain still. This game is dependent on how well kids can process the meaning and presence of the words before leaping into action or staying put.

Telephone

This one is tons of fun! Seat the kids in a circle. You can be involved or leave them to their own devices. The first kid whispers a starting sentence into the ear of the second child. It can be a line from a song or a story or even a tongue twister. The second child whispers what they heard into the ear of the third kid. This goes on till every child has heard the sentence and conveyed it to the next.

The last child announces the sentence they heard out loud. The final statement is almost always incredibly different from the starting sentence the first child whispered in the beginning. This game teaches how everyone has the capability of changing an experience. Their very presence influences the conversation from the first child to the last. The game isn't an activity with winners and losers, so the kids don't need to practice to be better at it. It's a simple but steely reminder that what you hear may not necessarily be what the other person has said and that it takes effort to really comprehend the original saying.

Strategy 5: Teach Clear Communication

Your relationship often denotes the kind of communication you have. Striving to speak in a straightforward manner means you value the relationship with the person you are speaking with.

Take this example: "Take out the trash."

This short sentence can mean many things. Should the child pick up the trash from the kitchen and drop it outside the house? Are they meant to clean up the kitchen and throw refuse in the trash can? Do you expect them to clean their room?

Without you setting up the right expectation beforehand or detailing the instruction, the child may go with the most obvious assumption (according to them). Ambiguity leads to pending chores, dirt piling up somewhere in the house, and rising tempers.

Clear communication takes effort. When we don't work to specify our meaning, we're leaving the instruction or conversation vague. It takes time to practice the skill of effectively conveying meaning and message, but once done, your child will be able to recognize any future ambiguity and work on their own to clear it up.

Communication Games

Every child or student should have a pencil/pen and a blank piece of paper for these games.

Picture Dictation

Compile a list of instructions beforehand so it's easier for you to repeat them if needed. State the instructions one at a time, describing to the kids what they must draw. For example:

"Draw a star at the top of the page."

"Write your name below the star."

"Draw a smiley face in the bottom left corner of the page."

"Scribble five random lines in the bottom right corner."

This exercise allows the children to learn position words, visualize the instructions, and then execute them. Give them good time to figure out these facets and draw properly before going in the next direction. This helps kids understand which parts of the instructions they have trouble with. Certain phrases could be difficult to understand, such as "bottom left" or "random." With practice, they can get the hang of the instructions.

Story Chain

Seat the kids in a circle. You can start the story by writing a sentence at the top of a piece of paper, such as, "Once upon a time…" or, "There was a cottage in the woods." Give them a setting or a character to kick off the tale.

The first student writes a few words or a statement as a continuation of your sentence. Give them a full minute to think and write a sentence. Once they're done, the next child adds to the previous text.

Thus, everyone gets the chance to write a partial or a full statement, building a story along the way. When all have finished, have one child read out the tale.

This exercise helps students practice their creative skills, thinking up a story and considering the style in which they write down the words. It helps if you set a theme for the story (adventure, sci-fi, humor). By having to build off of what the previous kids have written, this is a form of communication where individual students try to create a cohesive message that must make sense by the end.

Strategy 6: Praise Good Behavior

Positive reinforcement is a priority because it emboldens a child with the approval they need to accomplish a challenge or after completing one. Resorting to negative conduct, even to dissuade bad habits, can leave a lasting impact on your child that verbal attacks are acceptable in society, which they shouldn't be.

Types of Praise

Talent

Parents and educators offer praise based on what a child is capable of doing and how well they do it. For instance, a guardian may applaud their child for their drawing talent. But, without clarification, the child can grow up thinking their talent is innate and not something that can be improved upon. Simultaneously, other kids who hear this praise directed at their friend or sibling, and not them will believe that they are unable to achieve the same approval due to forces beyond their control.

Effort

When we praise kids for the effort they put into a task, we acknowledge the exact abilities that fall under their control. So, instead of praising their drawing skills, you can say, "Wow, that picture is lovely! You worked really hard with the colors, didn't you?"

This kind of praise can be given to anyone who tries their best at anything. It makes the lesson clear to the child that they will receive approval if they try harder, not if they're automatically good at a specific thing.

Behavior

Focusing praise on your child's positive behavior is an efficient mode of approval. This ensures the continuation of the desired habits in the long run. For example, you may say, "The way you've arranged your paints is really neat! Good job at keeping everything where you can find it easily!"

Here, the praise focuses on the things your kid has done in the correct or expected way. It increases the chances of them following that behavior consistently, knowing that they've gained your approval.

Deliver Effective Praise

Move away from personal praise and focus on the child's improvement in effort and behavior. The majority of their energy is aimed at these areas and thus, that's what your approval must target. The more specific you are about their actions, the better their progress will be.

Avoid going overboard with the endorsements. If you stick to sincere praises now, your child will grow intuitive in recognizing when they're given false wishes. The best kind of praise focuses on the child's process and trials. So, by avoiding comparisons between children, you'll boost the confidence and integrity of each child.

Examples of Appropriate Praise

- **Effort:** "I see how much effort you put into practicing your handwriting. That's great! Keep it up!"
- **Improvement:** "Your singing is much better than when you started! You did a good job of practicing so well!"
- **Kindness:** "I noticed how you shared your umbrella with your friends today. That was wonderful!"

- **Patience:** "You waited for me to check your friend's picture before yours. You were great at being patient!"
- **Responsibility:** "You cleaned up your table without being told. That shows responsibility. I'm proud of you!"

Strategy 7: Encourage Group Activities

You can organize a game with rules, such as a sport, for kids aged seven and above. They will be able to use the game's constraints to cultivate teamwork and fair play.

Team Sports

Participating in a structured sport such as soccer, dodgeball, or baseball helps children develop an understanding of working with others toward a common goal. They can learn to collaborate with their teammates and grow to trust and respect them. Playing a sport on a regular basis helps them stay healthy, which leads to better mental well-being as well.

Camps and Scouts

Joining camps and going in for the Girl Scouts or Boy Scouts lets kids traverse peer relationships in different social environments outside of home and school. They have access to outdoor activities, games, group projects, and even go on camping trips. The lessons children gain from exploring nature and the countryside go a long way toward encouraging them to respect flora and fauna. Beyond this, working on these projects teaches kids to contribute to diverse kinds of jobs, work as a team, gain experience from collaboration, and deal with responsibility.

Team-Building Games

Apart from regulated sports, you can have your students take part in scavenger hunts, tugs-of-war, relay races, and more. These games involve quick and direct team strategies that encourage professional and friendly bonding. If these games are conducted well, kids will experience the benefits of team contribution, leadership, guidance, and more.

Choirs and Bands

Students in grade school gain chances to be included in nonschool group activities such as children's choir and music bands. Strong peer inclusion improves communication and cooperation. Practicing vocal and instrumental skills helps kids develop better memory retention, greater emotional engagement, and higher creativity. These individual habits contribute to a healthier social life for children seeking acceptance in large groups carrying out a joint enterprise.

Community Service Projects

Group activities such as park and walkway cleanups, charity drives, car washes, lemonade stands, and book sales are more than the work itself. These are services where kids can understand the strength of the community, supporting people with fewer resources than them. It teaches children to help and show compassion for people outside of their close social circles. They will gain a new perspective from seeing other children and adults dealing with life problems upfront. Thus, kids will appreciate and be thankful for their safe circumstances and respect people from different walks of life.

Strategy 8: Teach Conflict Resolution

Conflict can stem from many reasons. One is an emotional disruption when kids cause an outburst that they find hard to explain. Another is a child encountering a situation that takes agency away from their preconceived notions of control over their world. No matter the cause, countering these disruptions can take some mental and emotional gymnastics.

You can motivate your child by having them think around the hurdle or out of the box. Ask open-ended questions that make them think.

Example One

You: "I saw you throw your toothbrush on the floor."

Kid: "I don't want to brush my teeth!"

You: "Why is that?"

Kid: "Just don't wanna!"

You: "Well, if you don't keep your teeth clean, you won't be able to eat your favorite snacks."

Kid: "No!"

You: "Why don't you like brushing your teeth?"

Kid: "The brush is bad."

By nudging your child to convey their experience, you'll get a handle on the problem's source. In this case, the brush may have been hurting your child's gums and causing sensitivity and pain. You can suggest brushing with their finger for the night and later purchasing a brush with softer bristles. This way, their hygiene is not compromised, and the problem is addressed.

Encouraging your child to engage in open communication with you reduces the risk of more conflicts down the road. And it's a long road, so being preemptive about any kind of disruption is a good idea. Along the same lines, you can help your kid develop new ways to approach anything they dislike but is necessary for them.

Example Two

Green vegetables are a perennial source of distaste for many young children. Your kid may throw tantrums and literally throw broccoli pieces off of their plate. The emotion is clear here: They don't like veggies.

Try this trick: Involve them in your meal preparation. For some kids, putting work into cutting up vegetables and watching you cook them brings them closer to the food. You can even change up the recipes and try something fun, like roasting the vegetables in various ways. There's a world of opportunity here to explore new spices and herbs. This method helps you and your child learn more about cooking across different cultures, and you may even stumble on a goldmine that suits your palate. When they're able to overcome the frustration by a noticeable degree, reward them with appropriate praise.

Other Conflict Resolution Tactics

Of course, beyond actually solving a situation, it's important to consider that some cases are simply out of your hands. If your child gets into a screaming match at the park about who gets to go down the slide next, you can't think of the situation as a winning/losing one.

Instead, you must regard de-escalation as a valid option.

Here are some tactics that your child can try to help clear their mind.

- Step back from the situation and take deep breaths.
- Take a hike! Quite literally, have them walk around in an open space to gain some distance from the situation.
- Count to 10. They can do this silently or out loud. Focusing on this helps reduce situational stress.
- Find someone else to spend time with. Kids benefit from walking away from disruption and finding others to play with.
- Try and work on it. Sometimes, kids can find the will to calm themselves down and hash things out. This is the result of effective communication and cool-down strategies.
- Find a trusted adult. A parent, guardian, or educator can help de-escalate the situation with immediate authority.

Strategy 9: Guide Them in Making Friends

As your kids blossom, they become more aware of life around them. Nature brings harmony, social outings bring community, and peers bring along potential friendship if the right kind of bonds are formed. Compared to grown-ups, kids make friends far more easily.

But not all of them find it smooth sailing. Friendships are as complex as the children involved, and there are skilled ways in which you can help these seven- and eight-year-olds form quick and long-lasting relationships with their classmates, neighbors, and playmates.

Friendship Skills

Use the introduction tactics learned in Chapter 2. Your child can simply walk up to a kid and introduce themselves by stating their name and then asking what the other kid's name is in return. Sometimes, that's all it takes to initiate a playful energy. Being friendly and open is a great way for your child to let the other party know that they are looking for a connection. Some kids like to play on their own, but many won't be opposed to a partner in crime!

Model Good Friendship

You can easily demonstrate the preferred kind of friendship you want your children to have. Bring in a partner or a friend and set a scene where you help each other with tasks around the house, such as planting seeds, baking, joining in hobbies, giving good advice, and the like. As stated in Strategy 1, observing model behavior influences children to mimic and imbibe the same traits into their daily life.

Consider kindness and gratefulness as your allies. Simply being polite to someone may not guarantee a trusted peer; you must show your kids how compassion and goodness register better. Guide them to share toys with other kids and lend a helping hand to those in need. Genuine acts of kindness are the way to go.

Schedule Playdates

When you put in the effort to secure the validity of a relationship, you get to reap the rewards. Playdates ensure that kids get to spend time outside of the regular schedule of siblings at home and classmates at school. You can invite other children whom your kids know and let them free in a playroom or a park where they can spend time conversing and exercising the freedom to simply run around, muddy and screaming. For a child, it doesn't get any better than that!

Temperament Sensitivity

Children's moods vary depending on the day and the events they face. And even then, their constitution is made up of very personal tastes, some of which we can expect and others that catch us off guard. This is the reason that some parenting tricks do not work: because they are not suited to a specific child's preferences.

Here's a good way of thinking about it, as explained in an article from Verywell Family (Kamenetzky, 2022):

Knowing your child's likes and dislikes is important to understanding how they socialize, says Lea Lis, MD, a double board-certified adult and child psychiatrist. For example, if your child is athletic or loves music, these are shared interests that can serve as the building blocks of their friendships. If your child has not developed interests like these yet, it may require a little strategic planning on your part to put them in situations where they can learn social skills. (paras. 12 & 13)

Strategy 10: Discuss Nonverbal Communication

Subtle tells, social cues, and nonverbal indications add a lot to communication. Reading body language is a practiced skill, and kids can learn how to do this by decoding emotional behavior within themselves first.

Position and Movement

Model the given movements to indicate emotion. Have your child repeat these actions or make their own movements to get a sense of how they exude emotion.

- **Happy:** smiling, laughing
- **Excited:** clapping hands, squealing
- **Sad:** shoulders hunched, sniffling, looking down or away
- **Angry:** scowling, folded arms, flushed face, stiff posture, clenched fists
- **Annoyed:** light frown, foot tapping on the ground, checking the time, sighing

Give Examples

Take the example of a good storybook that articulates a character's physicality when describing their emotions. You can also watch your child's favorite TV show and point out how the characters show their mood by using loud voices and very bold postures and movements. Recognizing these bold stances helps them connect nonverbal cues with spoken messages.

Body-Language Charades

Write the name of an emotion on a card and have at least five to ten cards ready for the game. Explain the rules of charades to the kids and let them take turns picking a card and acting out the emotion. Remind them not to use words! The other children must guess the emotion based on the body movements and noises the kid makes.

Exceptions

Remember to emphasize that not all movements indicate a specific emotional message. Someone tired may stretch their hands and yawn or sigh. This doesn't indicate any kind of frustration aimed at specific people. Someone else may rub their hands and cross their arms when they're cold, but this certainly doesn't mean they're impatient or angry. Let the children come to these conclusions slowly.

Strategy 11: Teach Patience

Kids born after 2012 and before 2025 are titled Generation Alpha. They're tech savvy, having grown up in the world of Wi-Fi, lithium batteries, wireless charging, AI tech, and more. Concerning social, economic, and technological trends, Gen Alpha is able to connect online instantly and gain answers to questions without having to contemplate too much. This 24/7 access to the internet has greatly reduced their attention spans and increased their need for instant gratification.

You may notice reluctance when coaching kids toward delayed rewards. That's alright. Demonstrate your patience in waiting for greater rewards, and they will be able to observe the connection there. Right now, the message is simple: Waiting ensures higher levels of gratification whose effects last longer.

Wait for Treats

You may have heard of the famous marshmallow test conducted by William Mischel's team. He worked on offering snacks and rewards to kids of varying ages and came to conclusions about emotional development and gratitude unique to different age groups (Mischel, 2014):

By age seven, children's attention-control skills and the underlying neural circuits are surprisingly similar to those of adults. The child's experiences in the first half dozen years of life become roots for the ability to regulate impulses, exercise self-restraint, control the expression of emotions, and develop empathy, mindfulness, and conscience. (p. 46)

You can try a similar setup. Set a marshmallow, a piece of chocolate, or a cookie on a table. Seat your child at the table and instruct them that you'll leave the room for 10 minutes. If they can stop themselves from eating the treat before the time you're back, they'll get an additional snack as recompense.

Remember to engage in positive reinforcement. This means if you come back and see that the child has indulged in the treat, don't scold them. Simply say that they can try again after a while (the next day), and remind them of the reward waiting for them if they succeed. Be firm in not giving the extra treat when they are unable to wait 10 minutes.

If they've succeeded in waiting patiently (or impatiently), praise them for their patience and self-control and offer the additional treat with a large grin!

Board Games

Certain games require time for the players to think up strategies or simply wait for others to finish their turns. This allows for extended family and communal time where kids can socialize with their parents and siblings outside of meals, chores, and other daily tasks. When it comes to school or third-place socialization, board games, card games, and indoor activities support similar emotional and mental engagement with peers.

Snakes and Ladders, *Monopoly*, *Life*, and similar board games allow for team building and individual direction. The multiple rules and guidelines may stymie your kids at first, but with practice, they'll be able to build up to playing the games with gusto.

Chess, Checkers, Go, Mahjong, and more are intellectually stimulating and can teach kids the benefits of strategizing and planning. Remember to praise your children for their effort and sportsmanship rather than just for winning these games!

Gardening Projects

Gardening is an excellent choice for children of any age. It takes a certain level of moderation on the child's part to stay diligent and patient while taking care of another living being.

You can start with fast-growing flowers and vegetables to show an apparent reward for waiting several days, such as:

- sunflowers
- morning glories
- cosmos
- peas
- basil
- cherry tomatoes

With vegetables, you get the added benefit of using them in your meals. Children will find greater satisfaction from the entire process of planting the seeds and then watering and caring for them till they germinate, flower, and give edible produce.

Strategy 12: Teach Respect

When setting up deeper discussions about diversity, bring in the people your children know who are dissimilar to them. Focus on the theme that dissimilarity *does not* equate to distrust. In fact, the more differences there are within a space, the more that space is populated with an incredible sense of community and connection.

Self-Respect

Keep communication lines open as much as possible. Let your kids know that they can reach out to you about anything that concerns them. Starting with respect for the self, teach them the beauty and uniqueness of being comfortable with their body and the way they look. If they wish to change certain aspects about themselves, it mustn't be because they're coaxed to fit someone else's idea of perfection.

Their body is theirs. Their mind is their own. Respecting your body, likes, and dislikes can mean different things to different people. Guiding a child to find euphoria in the things they choose and do is the best rule of life. Self-respect is essentially understanding the value of your own existence and your involvement in everyone else's lives. For a child, having to look out for their health and needing to stand up for themselves are some of the hardest, longest-lasting struggles they'll face well into adulthood.

Your directive is to simply stay resolute and nurture them toward practicing regular self-care: personal hygiene, regular sleep habits, a balanced diet, and proper R&R.

If you wish to ease your child gently into the reality of difficult decision-making, try puppet play. It's a successful method of expressing and handling tough feelings. Kids find it easier to channel difficult emotions and actions through puppets. Act out some of these scenes, where children must articulate their right to stay healthy and act against bullying.

- Someone tells a child it's alright to skip breakfast, but the kid stands up to them.
- A group of kids tries to convince another child to run down the stairs, but the child refuses.
- A group of kids pressures a child to take away a third child's pencil/hair clip, but the second child refuses.

Respecting Differences

Be direct with your kids. Talk about differences in skin color and hair type. Body positivity is a big deal since everyone will have thoughts about how their bodies should be and what megacorporations advertise as the "perfect" body. This is interlinked with race, gender, and body size. But, of course, finding acceptance in diversity involves varying religions, lifestyles, orientations, disabilities, and more. Approach these topics with your kids, knowing that they will already have seen many people with such dissimilar traits.

Sit with your kids and uncover various kinds of TV shows, books, games, and toys that boldly show and celebrate differences. Here are but a few explorations available to you!

Books

- *Under My Hijab* by Hena Khan
- *You Matter* by Christian Robinson
- *Sulwe* by Lupita Nyong'o
- *Say Something* by Peter H. Reynolds
- *The Sneetches and Other Stories* by Dr. Seuss

TV Shows

- *The Owl House* (2020 to 2023)
- *Kipo and the Age of Wonderbeasts* (2020 to present)
- *The Bravest Knight* (2019)
- *Blue's Clues and You* (2019 to present)

Games and Toys

- *LEGO Audio & Braille*
- *Barbie* (gender-neutral selection)
- *Ms. Monopoly*
- *Uno Braille*
- *Wonder Crew*

Respecting Rules

Rules are often spouted as suffocating constraints that stop children from having fun, but your responsibility is to dismantle this notion thoroughly. Explain how rules regarding specific scenarios are designed to help children and keep them safe. To keep things fair, all children and adults must follow the same rules. If a child is not allowed to stand on the kitchen counter, you must not climb up there either. Use a footstool or a stepladder to reach the top cabinets. This form of modeling desirable behavior was discussed in Strategy 1 and continues to be relevant here!

Find out the kinds of rules children are expected to obey and open a discussion about them so your kid can question why they're important. Oftentimes, children are not told why they must follow the all-important rules. A transparent conversation is bound to dispel reluctance and encourage kids to stay safe and vigilant.

Open a role-playing exercise that allows your kid to consider the consequences of breaking simple and dangerous rules:

- One child tells another that they will have fun if they skip school. Discuss how kids can refuse to do that.
- Someone tells a kid to cross the street without looking both ways. The child must speak up about road safety and diligence while crossing the street.
- An adult tells a child to cut a line. The child can discuss points on how to stand up to a grown-up and refuse to disturb queues. The solutions may involve finding a responsible adult to help out.

Strategy 13: Set Expectations

Behaviors have varying expectations in different social environments. We are vigilant and attentive on the roads, diligent and participative in class, quiet and busy in the library, and relaxed and comfy at home.

But kids don't get the memo right away. We must be the ones to let them know that, depending on the place and situation, their performance ought to change to suit it.

All the times you tell your kids to use their inside voices when you're at the library, to not run willy-nilly at the mall, or to not throw food around in restaurants are the results of them slowly experimenting and learning the expectations.

A Friend's Place

Now, a friend's place is definitely a house, but it's not your kid's home. It can take a while to get the message to seep in, so be patient! Your kids are just excited to visit their buddies.

We're revisiting Strategy 1 by exemplifying you as the model to follow. Some children may be nervous at another house and will look to you for guidance. It's the best place to start, and you can show how being polite and attentive to the hosts is the way to go. Your child can overcome their shyness by getting involved in games. The lessons of patience, respect, and effective communication are the major ones to keep a handle on.

You can practice this at home. Set up a fun tea party or a roundtable discussion of knights and warriors. (Both scenarios work for any gender; go with what your kids are most comfortable with!) Have keen discussions highlighting the importance of their manners in this scene.

"Wow, David. I like the way you helped set the table. Thank you for joining in!"

"Nice going, Alex! A genteel knight always remembers to share snacks with their team!"

Promise a reward for their good etiquette. Children notoriously improve by leaps and bounds, knowing they have a prize with their name on it! While this feels like a shortcut or a bribe, you can have a reward that includes the whole family, so make it an activity of comfort.

Public Space

Perhaps 10 years ago, going out to dinner was a simple event for you. Not anymore! When you bring your kids along, the night turns into an open-ended festival! Who knows how it's going to end?

You do. Or, at least, you will when you get a good idea of how to keep your little ones in check.

To be clear, we're not looking to have quiet and obedient children. We're aiming at getting our kids acclimatized to different surroundings and teaching what's expected of them out of the home. The lessons you impart tend to stick for decades.

Take these five points of courtesy to follow in a public space:

- **Use proper etiquette:** follow the rules, don't litter, and don't disturb others
- **Stay close to the group for safety:** This means parents, guardians, and teachers (for school trips)
- **Communicate helpfully:** Avoid yelling and pointing (unless needed)
- **Allow everyone to take turns:** share spaces and cooperate
- **Respect others' belongings:** Avoid messing with other people's stuff

Set the scene: You're at a restaurant. Remind your children that there are other people in the restaurant or diner. "If we want other people to be polite to us, we must be polite in return."

With that comes the entire baggage of active listening (to the waiter), patience (while waiting for the food), and respect (for you, the other customers, and the waiters).

Some restaurants offer paper menus with small puzzles and pencils to occupy the kids. But you can be a step ahead and bring some supplies with you. Of course, you may also be tempted to simply give them your phone. This is not inherently wrong, but while you're at it, have them play intellectually stimulating games and puzzles—or it could even be an educational video that teaches your kids while entertaining them.

For the children who can look away from the table and immerse themselves in the restaurant's details, you can play little games with them such as "I Spy" and "Copycat." This helps train their observational skills and lets them practice their outside voice to a degree.

Online Interaction

This Kidslox article underlines the reality of how young kids have a prominent online presence through app games and social media platforms (Bamford-Beattie, 2022):

According to research by McAfee, 67% [of] tweens (8–12 year olds) spend time on social media platforms, including Skype and Facebook. With millions of these digital interactions happening every second, playing nice online helps keep spaces safe and friendly for everyone. Teaching your child the importance of online etiquette is key to their well-being, both on and offline. (paras. 2–3)

Internet etiquette, or "netiquette," is the word of the decade. We can't simply order kids to stop going online. That would encourage them to weed their way into any device possible, and that's not what this lesson is about. Instead, we ought to teach them the importance of staying safe, valuing privacy, and practicing good manners while online.

When It's Online, It's Forever

This is the fundamental feature of the internet. We cannot erase embarrassing photos or comments online. We can take them down and delete our accounts, but people have the ability to download anything and save them on any server in the world. So, coach your kids to think twice before diving into online portals and platforms.

Privacy

Most websites require phone numbers and email IDs to register. If your kids sign up for games, documentaries, or social media accounts, contact information is needed. This opens up a way for the internet to reach back to them. Guide them on the value of keeping things close to their chest.

Teach Password Protection

It pays to be tech-savvy! Coach your kids on using strong passwords for their accounts. This involves the usual rules of uppercase and lowercase letters, numbers, and special characters while ensuring a minimal length.

Be Kind

Online interactions can become tense. Away from the website teams monitoring for trigger words, almost anything goes. Freedom of speech is a tactic used as a weapon to hurt others, but this is not something to be proud of. When one person shows true compassion toward others in a group, it can cause a genuine ripple effect and change the nature of communication into a balanced and kind one.

KIDS' CORNER!

This chapter lets your parents and teachers know how to help you figure new things out. The world is bigger than you thought at first. If you suddenly feel a little small, don't worry. You're not alone. Sometimes, even grown-ups feel tiny. That's why I'm here to give you some answers!

You get to be kind to people, to be patient, and to be aware of the different types of people around you. Share your games with friends, be patient, and let them take their turn. Listen to them when they talk, and they'll get the chance to listen to you when you want to stand up and sing!

And remember, stand up for yourself and your friends.

Have you heard of peer pressure? It's when other kids around you try to get you to do or say something you don't really want to.

I'll give you an example. Everyone knows lying is bad! But when your friend, who gave you a cookie during lunch, asks you to lie to your teacher, what do you do? Your friend was nice to you, but now they're trying to make you do something bad. Maybe that friend isn't so nice? It's okay to think about it. If you're not sure what to do, let your friend know that you need time to figure it out, and then go find an older student or an adult you trust so you can check with them what's the right thing to do.

It's hard to say no to a friend. Imagine your friend telling you to take a book out of the library without letting the librarian know. Yikes! Here's what to do if you're stuck:

- Take some time to really think about it. Is it something you want to do? The librarian took a lot of time to keep their books neat and proper. That's how you even found the book! It's arranged in the alphabetical order of either the title or the author's name. The librarian is really proud of their job.
- Taking the book without telling the librarian is against the rules. It'll get them annoyed, mad, and tired. What if everyone started taking books? What if someone took your favorite book? That wouldn't be fair to you.
- If your friend was really a friend, they wouldn't tell you to take things without permission. You could ask them why they need the book in the first place. Maybe they don't have a library card. That's alright! You can ask the librarian to make one and, trust me, they'll be happy to help you!
- If your friend doesn't listen, you can ask the librarian for help. Sometimes, they'll know about books that they can sell or even give away for free. Maybe you could take that one. But, at least you can trust the librarian to know what to do with books. It's their job!

When you respect others, you respect yourself. You are an important part of the way this world moves. So, remember: No matter how small or quiet you may feel, we're rooting for you! You can get better at asking questions. You can have a lot of fun even without cell phones and laptops. At times, all you need is to wait for a bit, be good to others, and, of course, be good to yourself!

SOCIAL SUPERSTARS EVERYWHERE!

"It is easier to build strong children than to repair broken adults."

— F. DOUGLAS

As you unlock more of my Social Superstar Strategies and begin to see the difference in your kids, you might start to notice more children around you who could use the same skills.

Even if your child has picked great friends, you might find one or two social skills lacking when they come over for a playdate – or you might simply wish that your child could use their new social skills to connect with more kids if only they had the same knowledge.

It's my goal to get these strategies into the hands of as many parents as possible. We all want the best for our kids, but we're contending with a digital world that we didn't grow up in, and most of us need a little help. So for the sake of parents everywhere, and for the other kids your child might encounter, I'd like to ask for your help in sharing these skills.

I know you already have a lot on your plate. Don't worry – this will take very little time. Getting a book into more people's hands is as simple as sharing a little feedback.

By leaving a review of this book on Amazon, you'll show other parents where they can find these essential strategies and improve their child's social skills.

Simply by letting other readers know how this book has helped you and what they'll find inside, you'll provide a guiding light through the tunnel of parenting children in the technological age.

Thank you so much for your support. Our children share the world with each other, and the more parents we can help, the better off all our kids will be.

4

REFINING SOCIAL SKILLS (AGES 9 AND 10)

Grown-ups never understand anything by themselves, and it is tiresome for children to be always and forever explaining things to them.

— ANTOINE DE SAINT-EXUPÉRY

Your child is nine going on ten, and you're wondering where the time has gone. This feeling lasts a while, so take a minute to let it seep in. It's necessary because your kid will be far too busy growing into themselves and discovering their place in the world and all the things they can do. There's no time to dive into nostalgic reruns of the past!

In this chapter, we'll focus on the more unique aspects of social activities and the subsequent challenges kids face. This is where they actively test out their social skills on their own with less prompting than younger age groups. Independence becomes a theme with kids of this age, who have learned to ride a bike without training wheels and begun riding out on the streets with their friends without you running after them.

WHAT'S IT LIKE AT THIS AGE?

By this age, children have gained clarity that has evaded them in previous years. They are able to think about the pros and cons of a situation, consider the value of secrets, and have in-jokes with friends and social groups.

This builds into an identity that they can call their own, a more flexible yet solid stance of who they are as a person. They form tastes and preferences that can last years or cycle through phases. On their journey to explore these likes and dislikes, your kids may withdraw from family engagements to pursue more peer-related ventures outside the house.

This need not be a failing. You can lean into it and allow them their space to explore while letting them know that they always have the option of approaching you. As long as they know to not cross the line between independent and self-indulgent, you can allow them this decision-making power.

You'll find them coming into conflict with areas of peer pressure, bullying (online and off), and general struggles with needing to be accepted by their friends and classmates. Sometimes, you'll need a nudge to provide them with the tools to handle things on their own. When you give kids the space to express themselves freely, they use their new words and noises to explain the racing emotions inside. The more they interact, the better they get at processing their experiences. This enhances their communication skills and, ergo, their socialization.

So, let's figure out how to get to the point of teaching children the rights and wrongs of social manners while giving them the agency to understand the world on their own.

SOCIAL SUPERSTAR STRATEGIES

Let's revisit how we can build on the 13 strategies to usher children aged nine and ten into carving out a nook for themselves in their social ecosystem.

Strategy 1: Model Good Behavior

Even at this significant age when kids try to be individualistic, your bearing has serious weight. By now, your kids will have learned to read subtle expressions from various people. They'll be able to catch you out on any disingenuous performance, so the best way to model ideal manners is to embrace them wholeheartedly.

You can make slight adjustments to your performance and convey way more than you could when your kids were younger. Modest changes in the tone, pace, and volume of your voice can indicate varying emotions. Focus on how you externalize your feelings to provide an example of how your kids ought to do the same.

Emotional Self-Regulation

By the age of nine, children find clarity in their complex emotional range. They realize that their feelings and reactions are more diverse. If not handled well, these emotions can become overwhelming. You can model your behavior and responses to help them recognize the variety of feelings and express the range of emotions in healthier ways.

Try a quick game with your kids. Your job is to describe your feelings and responses, and your children must guess the name of the emotion. Here are some examples:

- **Proud:** delighted about something or someone, rooting for someone, wishing luck for somebody
- **Bored:** not interested in the current activity, not willing to occupy yourself
- **Frustrated:** annoyed with something, not getting anywhere after putting in the effort, irritated by failure or rejection
- **Jealousy:** wanting something others have, wishing to be someone else just to get what they have, green-eyed
- **Focused:** attentive, aiming for something without distraction, paying attention
- **Compassion:** empathizing with others, showing kindness to others, acknowledging how others feel in a situation

By identifying these difficult emotions, your kids will be able to process them and respond to the situation more clearly.

Conflict Resolution

In a general sense, emotionally developing children get better at managing conflicts and problems around this age. Focus on scenes such as:

- Handling disagreements between friends

- Breaking something in the house but figuring out how to inform parents and clean up the mess
- Being transparent about homework, assignments, and studies

Social situations regarding the home, school, and tertiary places grow more layered at this age since nine- and ten-year-olds are able to gauge more complexities with the people, rules, and public fairness expected in close company. Your behavior models must approach these scenes with respect for others and responsibility for your actions.

Digital Citizenship

The internet is a wholly different playing field, widely accessible by anyone, thanks to the digital advances of all the devices we have lingering around our homes. Generation Alpha (children born between 2012 and 2025) is growing up entrenched in this media and tech far more than Generation Z (those born between 1996 and 2012) ever did.

But instead of fearing this outright, you can plan for it. If you're worried about your child hiding their internet searches from you, be open about yours.

Coach your kids on the rights and wrongs. Just as it's wrong to steal in the offline world, the same rules apply to the World Wide Web. Let them know that oftentimes there are other people sitting at their screens—real people with strong feelings who work hard to post their content online. Any attempt at hacking or illegally downloading information about people's work and identity is not just unlawful; it's unethical and truly hurtful.

Model transparency. Be candid about what you learn from the internet and give your kid age-appropriate information to help them safely navigate their online presence. In turn, they will be more forthcoming about their netizen role as well.

Critical Thinking

Many old-school subjects rely on rote memorization, where the child absorbs information and breathes it out for the exam. The better their memory is, the higher they score.

But this is a passive form of learning that doesn't strengthen the child's intellectual or emotional capabilities. By contrast, true, active rationalization involves reflective thoughts on the subject matter. When the child reads or watches information, their brain processes the data. Critical thinking will help them apply the information to their lives and reflect upon how the matter is relevant to them or others around them.

You can work on this with your child using simpler topics. Here are a couple of examples that can get you started!

- **Use soap to wash hands:** Fill a bowl with water. Sprinkle powdered black pepper on the surface. Coat your finger with a soapy layer and dip your finger into the water. Your child will watch as the pepper is repelled by the soap. Discuss the value of soap and water in disinfecting hands. The visual demonstration of soap cleaning things will spark fresh conversations between children.
- **Toss paper into the wastebasket:** This is a popular trick to teach in class. As a teacher, you can keep a wastebasket near your table or at the front of the classroom. Tell your students that everyone who can aim and throw a crumpled ball of paper into the basket gets to head off for recess early. This exercise highlights the difference between the experiences of kids sitting in the front compared to those who are at the back. Discuss fairness and the

importance of equal opportunity using this example.

Strategy 2: Role-Play

Group Projects

You may have heard (or experienced) how group projects become the bane of many students' lives when cooperation is not optimal. The moment a few members of the group choose to step back and let the others "lead," they essentially add to the workload of the ones who are actively working on the project.

Sample situation: Create a diorama of the cross-section of a volcano.

To drive home the exercise, the group members will have specific roles to play. The team will have a leader, an active contributor, a passive contributor, a disruptive member, and an indifferent member. Set a short scene where they discuss creating the diorama, but the leader and the active contributor speak the most. The passive member agrees to everything but gives no other input. The disruptive child interrupts the speaker with unhelpful jokes. And the last member does not participate in the discussion at all.

After the scene, you must highlight the points where communication failed due to a lack of active involvement from various members. The children will elaborate on these points, recalling how while certain participants tried to pull their weight, the entire project was bogged down by the rest.

Now have the students enact a new, short scene of them discussing the diorama, but everyone pitches in and listens to each other. This will demonstrate effective socialization and communication where every member is active and validated for their efforts.

Peer Group Dynamic

We'll cover the challenges and conflicts peer groups face in Strategy 8. For now, we'll have the kids practice discussing as a group where the skills of effective listening, clear communication, patience, and respect must be employed.

Sample situation: A group of friends must decide whether to spend Saturday completing their homework so they can enjoy Sunday or play on Saturday and leave work for Sunday.

You can monitor the kids as they figure out what they want to do, but the major points of communication must be evoked by them. Have them hash out the pros and cons of both arguments. Let each member speak up and vote for their preferred case. And, most importantly, keep the main point in mind: that the group must decide together and everyone should be in agreement.

Now if there was a tie-breaking vote, the kids who were part of the losing group must feel validated enough to agree with the winning side. You can encourage the kids to cheer each other up and continue the cooperative theme.

Social Gatherings

Anxious children can feel more prepared for social settings by role-playing those scenes in advance. Select appropriate scenes for them to build social cues and occupy their time well.

Example: Declare a birthday party where kids interact with peers and adults.

Set up three short scenarios for children to work with. Each one will test their patience, respect for diversity, and civility.

- **Patience:** Have the children wait in a long, slow-moving queue to get a piece of cake.
- **Respect:** Have each child explain the rules of a few games to other kids politely, especially those who may not be familiar with the game (noting that children from various cultures may have their own activities).

- **Civility:** Greet all kids and adults and treat everyone fairly. For example, show them the way to the bathroom, remind them to use the wastebasket, and make sure everyone has received beverages and snacks.

When you see children failing at one of the tasks, give them pointers on how to be respectful and polite to everyone around them. Have them treat others how they would like others to treat them.

Strategy 3: Teach Empathy

Kindness toward others must be genuine. Try to be as transparent as possible with your family and students without giving away your privacy. Your children will absorb the etiquette you set as they become their own people.

Handling Negativity

Let's look over a few instances that cause children to experience negative emotions. If we can coach our kids to manage themselves through negative moments, they'll grow stronger and more resilient to similar issues.

Rejection

Take the case of a sleepover. If your child hasn't been invited by a peer group to join their fun and fantastic sleepover, they're going to be rather unhappy. You must comfort them and let them know it's okay to cry and vent their misery.

Validation of their response to negativity is a helpful step in the healing process. They may face a case of FOMO (fear of missing out), so let them work through this at their own pace.

If the circumstances are benign, encourage your child to try again. Let them rack their brain and use a different tactic, such as offering to bring extra games and snacks to the sleepover. Sometimes their effort will work well, and the group will admire your kid's interest. But if it still doesn't work out, your child may be rejected again.

Affirm that your child's polite, kind, and respectful request did not work against them. Your child's personality was candid, and this requires your clear approval in order for them to accept that the group's decision was beyond their control. Praise your child's efforts and allow them the space to mourn the loss of a good time.

Jealousy

Give your child a clear, age-appropriate definition of jealousy. When you desire something that another person has, or when you wish you were in another person's place to experience their good fortune, that's jealousy.

First things first, provide your child with the space to feel this negativity, which can come and go in waves. Comfort them that it's okay to want a book or snack that someone else has. Rather than jumping straight to "solving" the issue, allow them to ruminate on the emotion.

Talk about an experience you've had so they're able to step back from their overwhelming mind space to see how others have faced this emotion as well. Give them a simple scenario: The bakery ran out of your favorite pastries, and you were jealous of the last person who bought a large batch of macaroons.

Guide your child through these steps:

- Accept that they feel bad.
- Avoid holding onto negativity. Find other activities that help them move away from the waves of jealousy and experience something else.

- Separate their *character* from the *behavior* of jealousy.
- Praise the actions they take to occupy themselves as a distraction.

Strengthening Empathy

Sometimes, it takes an outside intervention to help steer your child's decision-making prowess. Everyone needs a hype man! You can provide them with the space to work on their compassionate qualities. It's never a weakness to rejuvenate your empathy.

Books

Have kids read books and stories that emphasize offering empathy and compassion to kids and adults. This is especially useful when working with diverse experiences.

- *Save Me a Seat* by Gita Varadarajan and Sarah Weeks
- *Each Kindness* by Jacqueline Woodson
- *Lost and Found Cat: The True Story of Kunkush's Incredible Journey* by Doug Kuntz and Amy Shrodes

Movies

Visual representation of characters going on adventures while being kind toward their friends and family can affirm your kids as well. Let your child open discussions where they can talk about their favorite aspects of these movies:

- *Fearless* (2020)
- *Imba Means Sing* (2015)
- *Kindness Is Contagious* (2015)

Gratitude Journal

It helps to reflect on the day and find good deeds or moments when your child appreciates the things others did for them. Have them note down these moments of gratitude and encourage them to explain why they felt happy for certain actions.

Diaries and journals are a long-standing tradition in many cultures. But with the advent of technology, not many people put pen to paper and write down their experiences. So, when you suggest keeping a journal, let your kid know that there are multiple possibilities:

- Writing in an online notepad (chaperoned) to keep track of their thoughts.

- Drawing pictures, where the focus must be on the way they imbibe the elements with emotion.
- Writing poems, which allows for creativity to mingle with emotions, often inspires children to continue writing for years.

Service Projects

You can research charitable and community service places where your child can join group efforts to help others in need. A volunteer program is a good activity to teach about real-life fortune and the results of supporting people in times of crisis. Through this work, children of all ages gain a clearer sense of how the world works and how fickle everyone's life and luck can be.

- **Food banks:** Local support groups host food banks in and around many cities. This is a good place to educate your kids on the value of food and the merit of sharing it with people in need.
- **Animal shelters:** Many shelters hire youngsters to help look after animals they've rescued from the street. Offering food and safety, cleaning cages, attending medical checkups, and even fostering some of the animals can teach children responsibility and

how to care for those who cannot be independent.

Showing compassion to other less fortunate children, adults, and animals will guide your child to grasp the importance of sensitivity and kindness in the face of harsh reality.

Strategy 4: Encourage Listening

By this age, children are able to hold nuanced conversations with their peers, older kids, and adults. The best form of effective listening involves them understanding changes in tone and similar vocal cues and body tells that the speaker adds to the dialogue. Here's how you can coach your kid to notice these subtler conversational aspects.

Break It Down

Help your child listen to the vocal pitch and tone of the speaker. These facets can confirm if the speaker sounds happy, proud, sad, or annoyed. Connecting the vocal cues to the speaker's feelings helps the listener understand their emotional state faster.

Discuss Attitude

Describe what attitude means. It's a combination of someone's words, their tone, and their body language.

Demonstrate some examples of this to get the point across:

- **Annoyed:** Fold your arms, ask demanding questions, and raise your voice
- **Excited:** Cheer out loud, laugh, and clap your hands
- **Exhausted:** Massage the back of your neck, blink slowly, and lower your voice

Identify Inflection

Point out how children can change the meaning of words by altering their volume and speed of speaking. Demonstrate this with the question, "Are you still hungry?" with varying tones and emphasis.

- **Curious:** Ask calmly, raise your eyebrows to show interest, and emphasize the word "hungry."
- **Angry:** Ask in a louder voice, narrow your eyes to show a scowl, and emphasize the word "still."
- **Tired:** Ask quietly, give a deep sigh, show less interest, and give no particular emphasis

Watch Media

Select some movies or TV shows with great emphasis on character involvement in the plot. Examples such as *E.T.: The Extra-Terrestrial*, *Inside Out*, and *Firehouse Dog* work well.

Use dynamic character movements to identify scenes of sarcasm, sincerity, and teasing. The above-mentioned movies have various characters who show exaggerated facial features and strong body language when conveying emotion. You can use these examples to explain the characters' changing attitudes toward different people and situations.

Encourage Your Child to Question

There are billions of people speaking thousands of languages across the world. Sometimes, it's just not easy to pin down a speaker's tone or emotion based on their attitude or slang. You can encourage your child to politely inquire more about the speaker to figure out what their message is. Ask questions such as, "I'm not sure if you're being curious or sarcastic?" or "Would you explain what you meant by that last sentence?"

When they have the confidence to accept that they can work on their listening skills, the questions will come across as genuine interest, and the speaker will answer frankly to keep the conversation going.

Strategy 5: Teach Clear Communication

Now that your child is familiar with recognizing various body language tricks and vocal indications to understand a speaker's emotion, they can express the same cues to convey their own complex thoughts and abstract ideas. Beyond static words, the right kind of facial movements, body poses, vocal tones, and pitches collaborate to form an intricately constructed expression of emotion and meaning.

Metaphors and Analogies

Children love to exaggerate. They will find a few bees buzzing outside the house and announce that the bee army has been assembled to surround their base camp. You'll make their day when you give them the option of using metaphors and analogies to describe thoughts with strong sentiments like:

- It's so hot the Sun has to wear a hat.
- My math assignment can't be solved even by Einstein!
- My head is a scrambled jigsaw puzzle.

The types of metaphors they use will help them vent about the overwhelming aspects of a situation. Children can pour in strong emotions and embellish the description of their state of mind while still articulating their thoughts vividly.

Journaling

Offer your child the freedom to express their thoughts and ideas, and they will actively seek out new experiences to catalog in their journals. Writing about their feelings is a good first step to really deconstructing the root of certain complex emotions and the situations that caused them.

This practice helps children of various ages to explore and express complex sentiments. They will grow more capable and intelligible when translating emotions into words.

Assertive Communication

To assert yourself is to be confident and positive about your attributes. Teach your child the importance of being assertive about themselves and their loved ones. Situations that involve bullying or humorless teasing can be combated when kids stand up for their actions and words.

Body Language

Decisive body poses give children the confidence to speak up. When they make eye contact with the bully, they will be able to approach them as equals, willing to meet them head-on. They must also sit up straight or stand with their shoulders resting back and their chin up. Have your kid practice this pose. You can check that their body is not too stiff but alert at the right points.

Ideally, they should show a neutral face. Too much emotion often comes over as irrational and may escalate the situation. Confidence is about knowing how to handle the bullying as much as possible, not yelling over the bully.

Communication

If your child is confronting a teasing kid or a bully, they must stay as calm and collected as possible. A confident volume, neither too loud nor too low, is another ingredient of assertion. Your child should speak with a clear and firm will, their voice staying level and their words audible to all.

In some cases, the bully will be willing to listen and add to the conversation. In that case, your child must listen to them and not speak over them. It's a good resolution that everyone involved can converse effectively and that everyone's perspective is heard.

When speaking, your child can assert themselves by using statements with the word "I." So, instead of saying, "That book belongs to me. You can't steal it," your child will have better results by saying, "I own that book. Don't steal it from me."

This shifts the focus from the object to the child. By focusing on the fact that the bully tried to hurt your child (rather than just taking the book), your child asserts that they recognize the wrongdoing and do not condone it. By doing so, your child also emphasizes the bully's actions rather than labeling them as a "bad kid." This focus on behavior will nudge the bully into changing that behavior into something more appropriate. When children are directly labeled "bad," it reduces the chances of them trying to fix things outright and instead makes them focus on the hurtful label.

In the end, it's about gaining the confidence to refuse people the right of steamrollering over kids and exercising the right to say "no."

Strategy 6: Praise Good Behavior

Kids must understand what good behavior actually entails. When you ask them to complete a task, they ought to be aware of its details. For example, you may tell your child to wash the dishes. As long as they can find an appropriate footstool (so they are at a comfortable height with the counter) and know how to scrub the plates with the sponge or use the dishwasher properly, they won't have any technical difficulties with the chore.

But if your child doesn't know the amount of dish soap needed, or isn't sure how many dishes and vessels they must clean, or how to load the dishwasher correctly, we have a problem. Let's see how you can encourage self-motivation so your child is able to conduct good behavior without needless stress.

Build Confidence

Explaining the ins and outs of a situation and answering their questions will elevate your position in your child's eyes. They will see you as a team player who includes them in the game rather than just someone who's spouting out statistics and scores. When they feel involved, they will be able to trust their position in any circumstance.

Children who are outgoing and confident have been generally raised to be part of the solution and not just told the answers without their input. When they put their minds to work alongside yours, you strengthen their abilities.

Encourage Perseverance

It's not just about praising the good behavior you see; it's also important to motivate your child's efforts to accomplish it. Many children need careful guidance to realize their capabilities, and this is a tough journey for them. You must be cognizant of allowing them the space to explore and figure things out as much as they can while ensuring they stay safe throughout the endeavor.

For example, you can monitor your child's experimentation with the dishwasher so they learn how to clean up after themselves. As long as they don't cause electrical accidents or water damage, waste dish soap, or drop the breakable plates, let them work it out on their own. For the best results, you can show your child how you load the dishwasher and switch it on, and then have them replicate the process.

Promote Self-Reflection

With greater confidence, children find the strength to attempt new activities or more difficult challenges, knowing that you will be there to comfort them if they do fail. At this stage, failure is not seen as a complete loss but just a realization that their first approach did not cut it.

When children are able to seek approval within themselves, their psyche has also adapted to expecting praise when they perform certain tasks in the expected ways. Being self-assured by this is the result of consistent positive reinforcement over months and years. It compounds their routine and creates a positive feedback loop. They strive to live life with the qualities you've imbibed in them, expecting the approval that you deliver as positive reinforcement so that they repeat the behaviors you wish for. Except now, your kids are aware of the routine and consciously continue it.

Self-Discipline and Motivation

With strong self-reflection, your child will learn how to pursue positive behaviors and ensure good outcomes in general. They'll learn to cultivate discipline and even self-regulate their actions on a daily basis. With consistent praise for such behavior, your kid can grow to involve this in their everyday conduct even without the need for gratification, simply because it's part of the routine they've cultivated in their formative years.

Examples of Appropriate Praise

- **Improvement:** "I can see how much your math has improved over the past few months. All your practice is really paying off!"
- **Kindness:** "It was wonderful to see you stand up for your friend when they were being teased. That was very brave and kind of you."

- **Teamwork:** "You worked really well with your classmates on the project. You did a great job collaborating and sharing ideas."

Strategy 7: Encourage Group Activities

Learning cooperation skills at a young age helps kids to understand and work in social settings at a better pace. All through school, students have several opportunities to work together, be it in class projects, clubs, and PE games. This carries over to work-related projects, papers, and meetings that require multiple heads brainstorming.

You can favor group activities weekly, allowing children to pursue their skills individually and collectively. Try out these exercises, which train kids to use their collaboration and leadership skills.

Three-Legged Race

This is a popular one! The kids must pair up for this race. A guardian or a teacher will tie the left leg of one child to the right leg of their partner, essentially turning those two limbs into a single leg. Use a cloth sack to wrap around their legs so their skins aren't bruised from rougher ties or laces. At the signal, every pair must run from the start line to the finish line. The children must cooperate verbally and physically to finish the race.

Hand Knot

A "Hand Knot" or a "Human Knot" is a game where multiple kids stand in a circle and join hands with each other. Next, they move forward, crawling beneath other clasped hands or jumping over them. They must tangle themselves up as much as possible without letting each other go. Now, the kids must communicate and work together to untangle themselves from the knot without letting go. It's harder than it sounds!

Volunteer Day

You can host a volunteer day where kids help out in public spaces. Children can band together and assist in cleaning lawns and parks, serve hot meals, groom pets at shelters, and even aid reading communities in libraries. These activities allow them to form strong bonds, cooperate well, and help their neighborhood.

Nature Activities

If you live close to large parks and forest areas safe enough for group outings, here's your chance! Pack up the kids and go for a hike. The experience will be a rejuvenating one. The children can learn the rules of nature, avoid littering, and work as a team to trek through difficult trails while sharing food and water. Other activities, such as campouts and picnics, are great ways to spend time outdoors in good weather. Teach the children to enjoy the quietness of nature and appreciate the slow beauty the world has to offer beyond human life.

Strategy 8: Teach Conflict Resolution

Independent thinking is a developing feature in nine- and ten-year-olds. When it comes to dealing with dilemmas and arguments, you can try letting your child handle it and see how they use the strategies they've picked up so far to aid them in the situation.

Consider this: A group of friends has split into two sections over a disagreement. It may be a misunderstanding or a genuine issue, but how would a single child (who is unable to choose between the two sides) try to figure things out?

This child may experience pressure from both sections. If they do not make a choice, they may be shunned by everyone.

Major conflict resolution tactics involve the employment of empathy, patience, and active listening to come to an agreement or a compromise and mend relationships. You can walk your child through the following methods to figure out ways to reduce anxiety and dive into the problem with options.

What's in the Mirror?

First, take a look at yourself. Can you be candid about the ways you approach a problem? Children follow the example set by their parents and guardians. This touches upon our first strategy of modeling realistic and healthy behaviors.

How do you work out disagreements or misunderstandings? If your behavior is not the one you want your child or student to mimic, it may be time to shake things up. By admitting that you are willing to change things, your child will see the value in learning new lessons in life at any age, no matter the situation. This guarantees a stronger mindset and adaptability to various kinds of problems that they may never anticipate.

Remove the Heat

When it comes to the group disagreement example I mentioned, your child can think of the stakes in the equation. Is it time-sensitive? If the argument is about the movie they want to watch in class, there's a deadline looming over everyone, and that can make choices shaky. If your child has more time to appraise the situation, they should.

Let them take the extra time to hash out the specifics. This stage is not about arriving at an answer but about assessing which path to take. With time, your child will be able to grasp the tools they have at their disposal and approach the conflict with less duress.

Prioritize "Needs" Over "Wants"

In some cases, the need of the situation is not just to win an argument or even to solve the problem. It's to offer a peaceful time and space that validates everyone involved.

When offering options, bring the kids in. Let it not be a one-person solution. When you include everyone in the answer, you remove them from the circumstances of the problem.

Self-Assertion

It's vital to guide your kids so they find confidence from within and can assert themselves during difficult situations. Proper and consistent praise will help them understand how to go about challenging cases. It also helps them reinforce how to approach solutions and stick to their decisions in the long run.

Say the kids are arguing about the movie they want to watch in class. Your child (perhaps a tie-breaker) can suggest another free class in which to watch the second movie. Let them explain why they came to that conclusion. As a bonus, praise the movie choice and the section of kids who step back to yield temporarily.

The self-assured child will be able to propose answers or neutral spaces for others without second-guessing themselves. This is an incredibly handy skill to possess all through life.

Practice Reactions

You can role-play possible solutions with your child. Let them lead the practice sessions to see how best to portray emotion and body language. Confronting a disagreement is more about the people involved rather than the bare bones of a problem. While you can't prepare them for every possible situation, you can guide them to practice these responses:

- Stay in control of your emotions, and don't say anything you don't mean.
- Be confident and articulate.
- Avoid yelling or extreme shows of emotion.

Strategy 9: Guide Them in Making Friends

For some children, maintaining any form of relationship is as easy as breathing. But for many others, cultivating bonds is a daunting task. This Parent 4 Success article explains it well (O'Shea, 2012):

Every child has difficulties with friends sometimes, but some children are more inclined to have friendship difficulties. It may be that they are sensitive, impulsive, intense, lack concentration, or possibly that they have special needs or are on the autistic spectrum. For these children, it is vital to help them with this skill, or friendships will be a life-long problem. (para. 1)

While it's not easy to approach other children with friendship in mind, your kid can utilize the social skills they've picked up so far to achieve success. Here are some ways you can aid your kid to make and keep friends.

Observe and Praise

When you spend time with your kid, be it helping them with their homework or chores or simply hanging about the house, you get the chance to notice them puzzle things out. When the TV flickers, do they suggest replacing the batteries? When the doors creak, do they point it out? How do your kids notice and share ideas with you in their daily life?

Observing these acts gives you a baseline of their involvement. You can motivate their behavior by positively reinforcing their helpful words and actions.

Approve their actions when they put in a good effort to work on problems. Praise them appropriately when they share games or help others out.

Now you can let them know to use these attributes while reaching out to other kids at the park or at school. When they're able to use what they already practice at home, they're at a good jumping-off point.

Emotion and Sociability

Embodying certain social skills forms the behavior you want your kids to have in polite company. Careful socializing is about how they can deal with extreme emotions in a public space. It's not about hiding the emotional reactions; it's about understanding how there are things simply out of their control. Children take a while to digest that lesson, but it's possible!

Mention an example of you playing a board game with your friends and losing quite badly. Bring your kids into the discussion and mention pointers on fair play and taking defeat gracefully to congratulate the winner.

Be direct with your managed emotions. "I felt bad about losing. I tried so hard to win, but my best friend got the highest score. It's okay, though. I had fun with all my friends. And my bestie played a great game! I was so proud of them!"

The use of "I" reinforces the gravity of the situation and informs your kid that you have been in the position of accepting failure and still having a good time. They will have a better idea of how to handle frustration, knowing that you've done the same.

Children are resilient, but only up to a point. Give them the time to de-stress and comfort themselves when they've gone through a failing moment.

Define "Good" and "Friend"

Can children catch the exact features of relationships that are considered healthy, true, and uplifting? They can when they have a good understanding of what entails good social behavior.

You can show them visual representations of everything that makes a good friendship. Watch movies and TV shows with excellent character dynamics that focus on the traits of a strong and balanced friendship, such as:

- *Luca* (2021)
- *The Wizard of Oz* (1939)
- *Mr. Rogers' Neighborhood* (1968–2001)

Discuss the themes that these pieces of media explore. You can bring up the easy ones of kids introducing themselves to each other and sharing interests. And then there are the tough cases where a child has made a mistake and apologizes to their friends with a clear conversation or in a grand show of bravery.

You can make it an arts and crafts project! Select a favorite movie or TV show and pick out a strong and layered friendship dynamic to discuss. Build a poster or a collage with cards showing the names and behavior traits of the characters. Use colored cards to express the emotions of the characters in the scenes you want to focus on.

Sometimes, kids will be surprised by a piece of information you point out, something they hadn't noticed before. This is a good activity for children to put words to the various types of commitments they see on screen. Use the poster or collage you create to highlight the better and healthier bonds between characters that your children would likely seek out in reality.

Play

Properly done, playtime allows children to slip into a healthy mindset. Kids find greater chances of community bonding with their peers while also emotionally and mentally occupying them with games that help their physical activity.

Gather children in the classroom for some mood-lifting games, or round up kids at home for the same. Your children and students can also utilize their newly learned tools to form friendships and implement the games in larger groups. You'll be able to notice strong and weak interactions between some children and work on bridging the gaps wherever needed. And, if you're lucky, one outgoing child may rally the entire class into participating freely and equally, with everyone getting a chance to contribute and have fun.

Strategy 10: Discuss Nonverbal Communication

With the help of various types of visual media entertainment and properly observing family members interact, children, can get a good idea of nonverbal signs of communication. By the time they're nine, they'll be joining in this mode of conversation, including their body and space to convey mood and inject life into their words.

Eye Contact

Maintaining eye contact with someone during a conversation is more than just understanding the emotion they put into their words. In many cultures, steady eye contact for at least a few seconds is a strong sign of trust. It means neither party is hiding anything.

Their motivations are pure, and their conversation is frank and genuine.

This is also expected when we meet people in official settings. Perhaps you're seeing a new person at the office. It helps to maintain eye contact while introducing yourself. The gravitas of a person is detectable when they look into your eyes unflinchingly. Children understand that this is a power move, especially after all the times you may have stared at them, waiting for explanations when they've been naughty and gotten caught!

And, yes. Not all children and adults find this easy to execute. Many kids on the autism spectrum, those who are unusually shy, or the ones who deal with certain disabilities (such as blindness and deafness) will have a different set of milestones for understanding nuanced and silent types of communication. As mentioned in Strategy 10 of Chapter 2, you can give them little life hacks by training them to look at the middle of the forehead or right between the eyebrows of the speaker. Paying attention in this way still conveys good interest.

Stay Attentive

When your child isn't the one speaking in a conversation, they must still be attentive and hear out the speaker. It can be difficult for some who may have short attention spans or those who have symptoms of attention deficit disorder (ADD). When you speak to them, remind them to give you as much time as they can.

It helps if you model the ideal behavior of giving them your full attention when they're talking to you. Say, for example, they approach you for help with flying their kite, but you're busy working at home. Instead of continuing to stare at your PC screen while telling them you're busy, take a few minutes to handle the case.

Turn away from the screen and look at your child at eye level. Explain to them gently that you're busy at the moment and that they'll have to wait a bit. But you'll be able to join them at such-and-such a time. When you keep to your word and join them at the time you've promised, it reinforces the power behind the raincheck, all because of the way you conducted it.

Your kid will start behaving similarly, always striving to give everyone their full attention even when it's not 100% possible because, of course, they're a kid! You can give them some leeway in certain situations.

Expressions and Body Language

Facial appearance and body language can be very obvious and incredibly subtle, based on someone's attitude, inherent emotion, and the situation. Coaching kids to take notice of their own expressions and body postures aids them in developing a keen eye for others' non-verbal stances.

Walk them through some of them. You can model these examples and have your kids, or students guess the emotion behind them:

- **Surprised:** Raise your eyebrows, gasp out loud, and grin widely. Take a step back and look excited.
- **Puzzled:** Narrow your eyebrows and focus on one thing in the room. Tap a finger on your chin and look very lightly frustrated.
- **Distracted:** Occupy yourself with a task, such as reading a book. But keep looking away, perhaps at a clock, at a watch, or out the window. Tap your foot on the ground slowly, not in a hurry, but not focused at all.

Different Situations, Different Behaviors

Children are aware that their etiquette is dependent on their situation and setting. They're boisterous in a loud home, careful and attentive in school, quiet and focused in a library, active and participative in a playground, and courteous and careful online.

It always helps to go over the major aspects of what's expected in different situations. When you plan to go to the zoo, give your child soft reminders to:

- Not wander too far away from you
- Always stay in sight
- Be polite to others and follow proper conversation rules
- Avoid pointing at animals and people
- Not litter, but use the wastebasket
- Follow table manners and eat food carefully without spilling (remember to carry tissues with you!)

This is in addition to the usual rules of the zoo, which involve not yelling at animals or throwing food at them, and generally not antagonizing anyone.

If they are noisy or unrelenting at any point, remind them of the rules and encourage them to try their best. Some children find it difficult to contain their excitement and will run about to work off their energy. Just make sure they don't cause a ruckus and upset people. The kids will be fine!

In essence, remember to conduct yourself in a helpful and gentle manner. Your child will follow your lead most of the time and will strive to follow the rules as much as possible.

Strategy 11: Teach Patience

Instant gratification is when we receive immediate rewards for an activity. This involves no concept of waiting for answers or taking the time to solve a problem ourselves. Patience is becoming a rare commodity with the constant stream of content online wherever we look.

With the internet at our fingertips, we tend to look for immediate answers to everyday questions. Your children do the same. You may have heard of kids across the world simply checking the web for links to their essays, sometimes gaining the exact breakdown of a book's themes they need for their assignment. Your children will try the same, knowing that the internet has most of the solutions they need when it comes to regulated schoolwork.

Model Patience Out Loud

For example, social media offers short videos posted by content creators. Each one provides a burst of serotonin and the more we scroll, the greater our need for that feeling we receive the first time. And the more time we spend on this activity, the more our children see that we gain enjoyment from this type of content, and the more they'll be curious to try the same.

So, you must take prudent steps to demonstrate the clear value of patience despite technology stating otherwise. Here are some different ways you can model patience:

- **A slow half-hour:** Every day, perhaps early in the morning or after school, stipulate that for half an hour, everyone in the household stays away from screens and work. Host little games, perhaps with cards or a board game. Most activities that involve sitting down to think out strategies take time and can help dismantle the notion that speed isn't everything. Even if your kids try to opt out of the games, you must be fully committed. Perhaps you can spark their curiosity when they see you enjoying yourself without the need for any device.
- **A cookie jar test:** It's a tale as old as time. You set aside cookies for a week's worth of consumption, and kids try to sneak out loads of them before the day is even out! Instead of just telling them to take it slow, you can separate the cookies into separate tins, one for each member of the family. Then, prove to them how you (and your partner) enjoy your cookies way

more because you're taking it easy and having them once in a while. "The cookies aren't going anywhere but into your bellies. If you eat them one at a time, they'll taste better and last longer!"

Wait and Watch

The great failure of instant gratification is a lack of patience. When was the last time you sat down without your laptop or phone and simply watched the rising sun with a cup of hot tea? If you've done it recently, did you feel a sense of tranquility or unbearable boredom? This is the exact set of circumstances children are growing numb to when they're bombarded with a constant internet presence every day. Here are some waiting games children and students can try:

- **Hide-and-Go-Seek:** This classic game involves one person (it) counting to a large number and everyone else hiding. Once they finish counting, they must go around finding everyone. The first person caught will become "it" for the next round.
- **The Quiet Game:** This is a dreary tactic parents use to get some quiet time. But would you believe me if I said this can actually help children if you approach it differently? Get the

group together and choose one person to be the joker. The others must fill their mouths with water and hold it in their cheeks. The joker must tell a joke funny enough to get everyone laughing. The others must do their best to not laugh or spit out the water!

Notice and Affirm

Beyond instant praise, there's also the constant type of approval based on achievement, which does significant damage in the long run.

For many academically inclined children, a failing score is unbearable. You'll have heard of gifted children burning out. These kids have been so used to the praise they receive for being great at everything they try that when they encounter struggles, it's hard for them to accept failure as a learning point. To them, defeat is a terrible debacle that leaves a stain on their perfect report!

This, in turn, leads to many of them going for more tests and games, online or off. They may search for intellectual stimulation where their win is guaranteed. They'll find interesting games and not look back. The opportunities to spend time with family and peers dwindle when they search for help or entertainment online. It's simply not healthy for a child to fear and avoid the simplest of errors and constantly choose any sort of instant gratification just to regain that sense of "normalcy."

It may be an uphill battle, but you must shift their craving for praise by approving their efforts rather than their successes. It's possible. As an educator or a parent, you'll need to notice how their mood works based on your praise of their toiling efforts. When they fail at a task, be exuberant about their earnest work and the way they still put their time and energy into it. If done right, children will be able to spend more allotted time working on their task rather than abandoning it in the hopes of better and quicker results with the next one.

Strategy 12: Teach Respect

Self-Respect

When your child is able to affirm their own choices and feel confident about the space they occupy in a group, they are able to respect themselves. This is not about overconfidence. Self-respect is a level-headed understanding of your esteem and trust.

Open frank conversations about the following points:

- Does your child like themselves?
- What are their good qualities that they recognize?

- What are the good deeds and actions they've done recently?
- Do they feel happy and proud about these deeds?

If your child mentions some difficulties around feeling proud or believing in themselves, you can talk about their physical health and moods influenced by everyday events. Oftentimes, these facets of their well-being define their self-worth.

- **Collage:** Encourage children to turn their thoughts and feelings into collage work. Use photos from moments when they're engrossed in a hobby, working hard in a competition, practicing a talent, or any time they've simply been proud of what they've tried. This collage will be a celebration of their uniqueness and will allow them a deeper look into their individuality. Show them that their choices have made them into the person they are, and this will continue as they grow.
- **Arts and crafts:** You can have your kids try out different kinds of artwork—paints, pencils, digital, fabric, pottery, paper-mache, origami—that center around positive affirmation. Consistent repetition of sentiments like "I

respect myself," "I am strong," "I am a hard worker," and "I love myself" serve as daily reminders that helpful praise need not come just from a trusted authority such as parents, guardians, and educators; it can also come from within.

Respecting Diversity

Our beloved planet has more than eight billion human beings, with everyone part of their own ecosystems, cultures, faiths, and experiences. And with technology and travel, these cultures constantly clash and interweave. We have people with multicultural histories, orientations, races, disabilities, religions, and varying awareness of how vast and interlinked our worlds are.

Let's consider "Cultural Day." Some schools bring forth this option of researching a different country or state's culture to let the children explore its nuances and complexity. You can do the same at home. Introduce your children to independent movies and foreign films that can help familiarize kids with festivals or traditions they've never heard of, such as:

- *Spirited Away* (2002)
- *The Red Balloon* (1957)
- *Howl's Moving Castle* (2005)

- *Ta Ra Rum Pum* (2007)

You could even have a curated cuisine night. Once a month or so, prepare meals from a different country or culture for the entire family to try out. Be sure to be mindful of any allergy issues or foods your children absolutely won't eat. With these things in mind, there is a wide variety of options to choose from, including:

- **Shawarma:** This is an Arabian dish of pickled cucumber, tomato, onion, and roasted chicken wrapped in pita flatbread. You can add mayonnaise and hummus to the concoction.
- **Challah:** This is a Jewish bread baked as is or flavored with walnuts and chocolate chips. It can be eaten on its own or with side dishes such as hummus, feta cheese, jam, and soup.
- **Pho:** This is a delicious Vietnamese soup cooked with beef broth, vegetables, and tofu.

Respecting Rules

Every location and social setting has its rules, and children must be aware of their existence in any capacity. Most of these rules are in place to ensure everyone's safety in that designated zone. Children observe adults at work, so they'll notice your understanding of the rules and will mostly follow them. While rules help kids understand right from wrong, this is also the age when they will be exploring and testing out the legitimacy of any restriction.

As stated in the *Be Strong International Journal* (2021, para. 4), "This is what challenging behavior in children is all about. Children misbehave because they need to know just how far they can go before they face consequences. It's an important part of child emotional development."

This type of experimentation is quite healthy. Rather than raising children who quietly obey everything told to them, the strongest kids are the ones who test their surroundings. We must ensure that they do so, cognizant of the repercussions.

For example, a sign at a swimming pool may read, "No diving." Any kid who is tempted to dive is not necessarily someone who absolutely hates signs—they may simply want to test its veracity. Unfortunately, we know why that sign is put up. Stop the child before they get that running head start. Inform them that the pool is shallow, so leaping from the edge with full force will result in them plunging into the water and hitting the floor hard. This additional information will send them off annoyed, but they'll think twice about diving.

Show kids that the rules are for everyone. In general, regulations are not meant to single anyone out but rather ensure security for all. Engage children in these games to drive the point home.

- **Board games:** Friends and family-oriented board games such as *Monopoly*, *Clue*, and *Life* are great activities to encourage respect for rules. Board games have specific rules and steps to be followed. They also help children learn about taking turns and fair play.
- **Sports:** Field activities and sports such as soccer, volleyball, and tennis are great tools for teaching the importance of rules. Each sport has stipulated regulations on what the players are allowed to explore. These rules must be adhered to so everyone can play fairly and score well. Respect for sport-based rules can translate into equitable comprehension of rules in other areas of life.

Strategy 13: Set Expectations

Handling Differences in Public Spaces

Children must remember to value differences—visible or not—in people. They might see people with very different hairstyles and skin tones. They'll come across citizens wearing incredibly diverse clothing, the likes of which your kid may not have seen before.

Instead of boldly (and rudely) pointing at others, they can either be polite and ask people about crutches, walking canes, wheelchairs, and prosthetic limbs or simply not say anything. Implements ranging from inhalers to colostomy bags must be treated with respect, even when not understood. If people use them and are dependent on them, these objects are absolutely vital!

Benign curiosity is harmless and can even be sweet. But the line between curiosity and nosiness is sometimes illegible, and it pays to take notice of when words or actions move away from jesting to downright awful bullying.

Sometimes, differences can be incredibly subtle! A barista with cochlear implants may rely on partial sounds and can read your lips very well, but that doesn't mean they're suddenly fully able with no need for medical reference or help. We have the power to raise a generation who allow each other to venture into the world and not feel so attacked. Everyone is out just to have a good time.

Online Interactions

Yes, the web can be scary, but the world has always been terrifying in a multitude of ways, and the internet brings that reality to our doorstep. You can hold your kid back from accessing the online world as much as possible, but they will find a way behind your back, and that's perhaps the worst approach to the situation.

Let them know that you'd like to help them set up a few things so they stay safe while having fun.

- **Passwords and privacy:** Signing up for website accounts (be it games or social media) always involves a risk factor when we input some type of contact information. Convince your kids to use strong passwords to secure their accounts. Avoid giving away personal and contact data as much as possible.
- **Avoid stealing and hacking:** Some websites have harmless clickbait, and then there are those with silent viruses waiting to strike. Often, certain games and apps cost too much, and the tempting offer of free downloads can weaken the greatest of resolves. But these can be the perfect Trojan horse! Avoid things that seem too good to be true and too easy to acquire. At the risk of shattering your child's

wide-eyed gaze through their rose-tinted glasses, it's important they know the consequences of accidentally downloading nefarious viruses or even taking copyrighted data.

KIDS' CORNER!

Chapter 4 is all about the things you get to discover about yourself, your friends, and the world. You're stronger than you think. And thinking is your new superpower!

Thinking for Yourself

Being able to ask the right questions and understand the world better is a great lesson. When grown-ups say "critical thinking," they mean to check if you know things because someone told you about them and you just believed them or if you questioned about it to understand better.

Sunflower seeds give us sunflowers. Well, we know that. But how and why does it happen?

Bring some friends or siblings in on this! Get a few sunflower seeds and plant them in a garden. Take care of them. Water the seeds and make sure they get enough sunlight.

It will take a couple of weeks for the seeds to germinate and flower. Each seed has the amazing ability to grow into a tall plant with a large sunflower. And each flower has hundreds of little seeds right in the middle! What do your friends think about this? Talk about the seeds visible in the large sunflower that sprout after weeks of care. This is how a lot of plants continue their life cycles using sun, water, soil, nutrients, and time.

Understanding Diversity

Understanding and respecting people from all walks of life is not all that difficult. Remember, it's not necessary to learn *all* the experiences possible. There's a lot about life and people you'll never find out. A boy growing up in a small town in Nebraska would be pretty wowed if he saw the life of a girl living in a high-rise in the middle of Singapore. A kid from Hong Kong who's pretty sheltered would be super stunned to watch a paraplegic teenager playing basketball in Toronto.

And this is alright! When you respect other kids' experiences, you'll get to know how amazing and different everyone is.

Real-World Socialization

You probably have a high score in some of your favorite games, and that makes you feel pretty swell. But sometimes, when you're looking for fun, it helps to put your phone down and meet your friends face-to-face. I got the same advice from many of my friends when they wrestled me for my cellphone, that's for sure! I'm always happy and floaty when I spend time with them outside the house. It's alright if you can't always play with large groups of friends—spending time with even a few of them is a brilliant way to make you feel like you're flying!

Even if your friends are busy, you can still get some chill time. Balance out your online socialization with equally strong offline stuff. For every hour you play on an app, take the time to get out of the house. You can walk your dog or tend to the garden. It's not easy at first, but I promise you, it's worth it!

You've got a great head start to figure out how to work on these social skills. In the next chapter, we'll look into the world of preteens and see what lies ahead. It's an even bigger landscape for you! Remember, you have all you need to set off on this adventure of growing up.

5

TRANSITIONING TO ADOLESCENCE (AGES 11 AND 12)

When we give children advice or instant solutions, we deprive them of the experience that comes from wrestling with their own problems.

—ADELE FABER & ELAINE MAZLISH

Tweenage time. Kids aged 11 and 12 are right on the cusp of puberty (on average), simultaneously treated like small children and "unruly" teenagers. But adolescence is fast approaching, and rather than fretting about the unspeakable horrors of preteen socialization, we can embrace them (both the horrors and the kids).

In this final chapter, we recognize the independence set forth by children looking to define their personality not only in relation to their family but also to their friends and other social peers. This is where the world is invited into their social circles. So let's prepare them for what's to come.

WHAT'S IT LIKE AT THIS AGE?

Eleven-year-olds are not only better equipped at reaching out to peers than younger children, but they also consider friendships as the more important part of life. Most kids will have a bestie or a very close group of friends comprising neighborhood kids or classmates. At the very least, these children prefer like-minded people.

This is also about the time when some children start to gain fluttery feelings for each other. You may notice your kids either running away from children of different genders or magnetically drawn to them. Based on all the TV shows or movies they've seen, kids try to connect these new warm sensations to their experiences. Let's check on our strategies to figure this out.

SOCIAL SUPERSTAR STRATEGIES

Here's the next avatar of the 13 tactics to guide 11- and 12-year-olds into the broader scope of socialization.

Strategy 1: Model Good Behavior

With sufficient socialization, children are eager to form strong connections, experience deep feelings, and grasp a diversity of perspectives. Often they encounter childish treatment from older kids and adults that contrasts with the inner turmoil of feeling "too old" for certain stories, toys, and games.

You can model socially approved behaviors to help them cope. If you can instill diligent behavior in their early life, they will tend to stick to the routine in their teenage years, as well as beyond.

Responsible Behavior

- **Be punctual and neat:** Make an effort to be on time for everything. Keep your living space moderately neat. When we direct our kids to look out for their hygiene and mind the time, we must be aware that it's not the easiest thing to do. When they see us trying our best, they will strive for the same. Remember to praise them when they work hard at it!
- **Take responsibility for your actions:** If you're somehow late to your kid's soccer game due to traffic, apologize gently and say that you're proud of them for waiting so patiently. If they find your messy table, let them know that you

need more time to clean it up. In essence, explaining your reasons keeps your children in the loop. You're not just a parent who picks up after them; you're a person with your own responsibilities and flaws.

- **Keep your promises:** Consistently performing this obligation ensures your child gets the message that their word is important. If they promise to finish their homework before heading out to play, you can rest assured they will do so since they've learned that reliability from you.

Managing Emotional Outbursts

Allow your child the chance to observe the way you handle turmoil well.

- **Avoid extreme reactions:** Frustrating events breed greater aggravation if unchecked. Some adults may be merely annoyed, but others may scream and yell in anger. Even if they calm down quickly, the damage may be done, especially if their child witnesses the adverse reaction. Kids are wont to mimic their parent's behavior and thus may also scream out any words they've heard in their parent's tirade.

- **Maintain composure:** Show them how you manage out-of-control situations. For instance, you may tell them about the time you were working in the garden when you forgot to check the time and the automatic sprinklers turned on. You ended up completely drenched and muddy! Tell your kids (or, better yet, demonstrate clearly) how you took a few minutes to breathe slowly and say, "Yep, you're probably wondering how I got like this. I spent way too much time on my gardenias and ended up soaked!"
- **Express emotions appropriately:** By appropriate, I mean you can show how you respond to something unusual or bad. The first step is to avoid an extreme reaction, the second is to take the time to maintain composure, and the third is to outwardly show a more considerate form of venting. As an adult, you hold obvious authority over children (especially those who are dependent on you). Thus, you must be careful of your expressions since they will affect the watching kids.

Drenched by sprinklers? Once you stop yourself from yelling or kicking things around, take deep breaths and announce that you need a short break to get cleaned up and vent appropriately.

I have a friend who speaks like a Victorian lady when she's frustrated: "This change in events has displeased me so! My notions on antiquated rituals aside, all I wished was to harvest my glistening tomatoes. Yet here I stand, innocent and wronged, soaked to the bone thanks to these devious water sprinklers. Oh, how the 21st century mocks me!"

It never fails to tickle any listener's fancy!

Dealing With Peer Pressure

Sometimes putting emotions into words helps reduce miscommunication. It can also boost confidence and allow kids to stand up to well-meaning or more malignant bullying. There's a fine line between being teased and feeling incredibly uncomfortable. When dealing with peer-enabled pressure, children may panic and go along with it to conform to their social group.

Here's what you can try to get them to rethink that social duress. Share real-life examples of when you stood up for your values, even when that singled you out.

"I don't like the idea of jumping across the ditch. Let's do something else!"

"If you can't have fun without teasing others, then maybe I should go hang out with the others."

Help them state their discomfort boldly. They must sound confident and be proud of their stance to not partake in that form of unpleasantness.

Handling Conformity

Aside from bowing to peer pressure, conformity leads to behaviors that can fundamentally change a child's character. It's important to reach out and address the fear kids have of being anxious or asocial if they aren't accepted into a group.

- **Focus on their individuality:** Every child is unique, which allows them to perceive beauty in differences over similarities. You can bring up the distinct features about yourself that you're proud of. Hold a conversation with your child, letting them point out their individuality with pride.
- **Respect their own differences:** Exploring self-respect involves the child valuing physical and psychological differences. First, focus on your differences: skin color, hair type, faith, orientation, or physical features such as eye color and nose. Tell them how you love the idea of standing out in a crowd and how there is

comfort in not necessarily blending in. Use anecdotes to prove the strength of diversity.

Strategy 2: Role-Play

Kids aged 11 and 12 are more involved in social experiences with their peers, exploring online, offline, platonic, and romantic bonds. Use examples to demonstrate how to manage social atmospheres concerning these new areas.

Social Media Responsibility

As much as there is incredible fun and amazement to social media, the drawbacks must be emphasized as well. People are essentially protected by a virtual barrier when they post blogs, articles, and comments online. But this often increases the distance between us and precludes genuine humanity. It often feels as though we're not conversing with a person who has real feelings that are hurt by rude comments. This is often the case when we don't meet these people offline or even engage in a video call.

Say, for example, your child finds a rather funny online comment about a friend, but you see the rudeness of the words that float over your child's head. You'll need to sit your kid down and explain that social media can host hurtful messages like this.

"See how this joke makes fun of your friend? It means the joke isn't nice and could hurt them if they saw it. Since you're a good friend, you can avoid sharing the comment or post."

Once this is described, invite your kid to role-play the scene of them supporting the friend who's hurt by the rude joke. This will test their empathy, compassion, respect, and patience.

Handling Romantic Feelings

Healthy milestones aren't determined by age but by the child's environment and character. By the time they're about 11, your child will tend to focus not only on platonic peer relationships but on romantic ones as well. This is not the same for all, and there is certainly no specific age of revelation. Simple attraction and genuine crushes can range in intensity.

Your support must ensure that they are able to handle the confusing new feelings without fearing peculiar retribution. It helps to demonstrate scenarios where you articulate the emotions of a child with a crush. This way, your kid can find the elements they can relate to and grasp the ones they can't understand at first.

This involves a complete and fair acceptance of the kid your child likes and how intense the attraction may be. Be aware that if your child is attracted to someone of the same gender, they may hide these feelings from you for fear of a negative reaction.

Thus, your express responsibility is to react calmly and without prejudice. If you need help with this, reach out to someone who you and your child trust to talk to about these matters. The goal is to provide reassurance to your kid.

When you role-play the scene describing a crush, make sure to touch upon these points:

- **Communicate emotions:** Describe the adrenaline rush of "butterflies in your belly" or the warm feeling that some might get. You can pull from your own experiences if it's age appropriate. Bring up uncomfortable sensations as well, such as nervousness and sweatiness.
- **Understand boundaries:** Crushes can often be just a one-way street. Your child may have a long-standing crush on a good friend, but if the friend doesn't reciprocate, it can cause a lot of distress. Rejection is never easy to contend with, and kids can be rude when hurt badly. You must emphasize the need for politeness and kindness even in the face of such rejection. Your kid should be able to respect others'

boundaries and must not push or provoke anyone who rejects them.

Strategy 3: Teach Empathy

Empathy allows children to really swallow their egos and step into another's shoes. They accept that not everything is evident in the world and are ready to learn about the experiences of others to gain a better understanding of them. An excellent bout of empathy allows kids to develop strong relationships with each other and the adults in their lives. They will be able to grasp the presence of differences between people and groups and accept these differences. This leads to a reduced inclination toward relentless teasing and bullying.

Positive Role Model

We always circle back to Strategy 1, which shines a spotlight on the importance of modeling positive behavior. Demonstrate your willingness to help others with no reward to yourself. Show your children that this type of behavior is something that can be cultivated slowly. Be kind to your neighbors, friends, and family. Acknowledge and accept the differences in people.

Reminisce About Moments of Kindness

Think back to a time you remember your child helping someone out, or perhaps they were assisted by somebody else. These are real scenarios that carry weight. You can use them as teaching moments to help your child grasp the deep value of compassion. These unexpected moments are a great reminder that empathy works at all levels.

Even if it's as simple as lending someone a pencil in class, the emotions evoked at that moment are indelible. Beyond simply discussing these memories, you can find photographs of heartful events to drive the point home. Or, your kids can even sit down with arts-and-crafts supplies and create little souvenirs of these moments of kindness.

Encourage Historical Empathy

Look beyond your children's lives and search for famous and not-so-famous stories of excellent role models showing kindness throughout history. One of the best examples is the late Diana Spencer. She was famously known to be generous and kind to patients suffering from AIDS and leprosy. She saw the people behind the pain and not just the diseases that scared many others. She demonstrated how accepting differences—especially those that people simply didn't have control over—was a matter of mind over intolerance.

Essentially, when we respect diversity, there is harmony among people of varying lifestyles. We interpret life and how to live it in our own styles. Basic dignity affirms our comprehension of the world. Just as a child must be free to choose their career based on their potential and limitations, they must afford the same respect to the people around them!

Strategy 4: Encourage Listening

Listening goes beyond hearing words. There's a significant difference between simply registering that your ears detect sounds and your brain genuinely processing the sounds to make sense of the speaker. So, when we consider active listening, inform your children how a good listener understands the meaning and emotions behind words by taking the time to focus on really listening to their friends and teachers talk.

Full Attention

Excitement interrupts manners, but this is an entirely forgivable offense if children are able to understand how emotions can change their response if they are not managed. So, when we encourage our children to listen, they must be able to pour focus into the active state of hearing people out. State it very clearly to them:

"Give your friend complete attention. They have something really important to tell you. If you listen well, that's a start to a really great conversation because they'll listen to you too."

This shines a light on how an active listener shows real interest not just in having a conversation but in the speaker as well! It strengthens the relationship between the listener and speaker in the long run.

Talk Without Interruption

When your child listens to a speaker, they must exercise restraint over their own speech. Avoiding any kind of interruption—however well-meaning it may be—offers the speaker greater agency to offload their perspective as a whole. Thus, it contributes to a better communicative atmosphere where the message is not lost at any point.

Even if your child has doubts about the topic or needs answers to questions, teach them to hold these thoughts in reserve and wait for the speaker to finish. In most cases, the speaker will unknowingly answer the doubts or queries, but it's also important to not break their train of thought. This is especially crucial if the speaker is young and is working off of a stream-of-consciousness format.

To best embed these traits in your children and students, model this behavior of actively listening when kids have a large speech to spout. It takes patience and effort, and that is the point!

Strategy 5: Teach Clear Communication

When kids are able to efficiently listen to their peers and adults, they will be able to hold lucid conversations with no misunderstandings. In addition to this, it's vital for them to know how to change the status quo of a conversation by having to disagree with their friends or apologize for something relevant, be it face-to-face or online.

Disagree Respectfully

It's frankly not possible to go through life agreeing with everyone. Moreover, raising kids to say "yes" to everything is a dangerous notion. In fact, when done well, disagreements are respectful and help build communication and collaboration skills. It keeps conversations alive and shows how people with varying opinions can still come to a satisfying conclusion.

Teaching children to express their contradicting perspectives contributes to a diverse society. In both physical and virtual interactions, cultivating respectful disagreement allows kids to listen actively, consider varying ideas, and find common ground while appreciating differences.

Show how to express disagreement constructively. Avoid resorting to personal attacks. It helps to focus on the issue at hand rather than targeting the individual. Here's a scene you can role-play with your child or with a group of students:

Child: "I added the first and second numbers before multiplying the sum with the third number."

You: "I see. But your answer is wrong. You did well with the other problems, so let's focus on this. Use the PEMDAS rule."

Child: "But I already got the answer!"

You: "Yes, you wrote down this number. But look here. The rule states you should multiply the second and third numbers before adding the first to their product. Try again. You'll get it right!"

This can either be you or another student guiding the first child toward the solution. The trick here is to show that the method was wrong, not the child. The child always has room to grow, while the wrong method remains wrong. Coach your kid to respectfully disagree with wrong opinions because it allows for open dialogue between people.

Apologize Sincerely

Learning to apologize genially is a fundamental life skill. Apologizing helps children recognize the impact of their words and actions on others. They are, thus, able to foster empathy and accountability. Moreover, it strengthens relationships by promoting forgiveness and understanding.

An apology must be more than direct words; it should be an authentic expression of repentance. Understanding the importance of acknowledging mistakes helps kids take responsibility and make amends.

Regardless of the communication medium—online or off—a genuine apology involves these ingredients:

- **The exact issue:** Your kid must know the actual issue of the apology. When they say "sorry," it must refer to the action or words that caused harm in the first place. This shows the child is aware of the hurt they've caused, intentional or not. Taking responsibility for their behavior is a sign of empathy that we desire in all children.
- **The right reason:** Your child ought to understand why the issue was an issue in the first place. By recognizing the hurtful parts of the exact issue, they can apologize and

understand how certain problems affect various people differently. This type of awareness shows your child comprehends nuance and has the self-control to acknowledge the problem and grow as a person.
- **A possible resolution:** Providing potential answers to the problem or trying to make amends are true signs of kindness. Your child recognizes that the situation is not about them but about the people who have been hurt. This can be simple, for example, if your child can promise to not behave discourteously again. It can be tough in that your child must be involved in cleaning up the mess they had a hand in creating. But taking this responsibility ensures that they are now part of the solution and not the problem. Helping people will build trust in relationships.

Communicate Online Appropriately

Online presence and communication are a staple in our lives. Our children grow up in this world far more adept at it than us. So it's absolutely vital for them to understand that disagreements are a constant theme online, while apologies are sorely needed.

Lessons on the importance of empathy and patience work best here. When kids express their thoughts online, it must include clarity and remorse to reduce friction. Yes, online communication is a big deal for social and emotional growth, so you must be able to guide your child well enough to get them through the more difficult conversations online.

Online communication ranges from direct text messages and voicemails to public comments on popular posts. When we consider the weight of the internet behind every video call and DM, *caution* is the word of the year. Most times, we are not privy to people's faces behind their blogs and accounts. That lack of facial expression or vocal tone lends itself to different communication rules.

And this grows doubly frustrating when disagreements pop up. Remind your child that online interactions may seem disconnected from the real world, but there are genuine people behind the posts and comments. Encourage them to use polite language as much as possible. It should be clear when they can use sarcasm in informal settings and when that must be avoided. Use simple online texting rules to ensure messages are not misunderstood.

- Typing in all capital letters indicates you're yelling. Kids can use this to show excitement between friends.
- Avoid using an ellipsis to end a statement. It indicates annoyance and can put the reader off.
- Understand what emojis and abbreviated exclamations really mean before using them. For example, LOL is "Laugh Out Loud" and not "Lots Of Love"!

The above samples of "netiquette," or internet etiquette, help give you an idea of the things to look out for. Your kid may already know some of this, but it never hurts to reinforce the importance of maintaining respectful online communication.

Strategy 6: Praise Good Behavior

Positive Affirmations

Everyone has a type of internal monologue. This may be a visualization of processing information, or it can be an intangible voice. The monologue, or self-talk, can veer toward positive aspirations or sink into negativity. Ideally, if we can guide our kids to encourage positive self-talk, they can grow to be optimistic and inspired by their own skills.

Self-affirmations are phrases that boost our esteem and confidence. Statements such as "I am strong!" and "I can do this!" help people of all ages to continue their journeys of self-discovery. Here are some examples of how to turn negativity into positive self-talk:

- Avoid, "This is too difficult for me." Try, "This is challenging, and I want to try it!"
- Avoid, "I'm bad at math." Try, "Math is difficult, so I need time and help to work on it!"
- Avoid, "I fail at tests." Try, "I will study and get better scores than last time!"

When we inspire our children to consciously choose to be positive, they'll start to approach difficult situations feeling motivated. Optimism can raise our self-confidence. Instilling this from a young age will help your kids propel themselves even when others around them have negative opinions.

Induct the following affirmations into your child's daily routine. Let these statements be the first thing they say to themselves in the morning:

1. Every day is a new beginning.
2. I have the ability to make good choices.
3. My voice matters.
4. The space I take up is good.

5. I am hard-working, brave, and _____. (Add an adjective the child aspires to be.)

Counter Negativity

If your child can recognize the difference between negative and positive self-talk, they can actively avoid being negative and purposefully think positively. This helps improve their mood and self-esteem. But combating negativity can be a tough act.

Here are some examples of such self-talk:

Negative	Positive
My handwriting is bad.	I can improve my handwriting.
I am not great at making friends.	I can learn different ways to make friends.
I have to speak in public next week, and I'm not ready!	I have to speak in public next week, and I have the time to practice my speech.

As you can see, the traits of negative thoughts highlight flaws and shortcomings, while positive thoughts do not disregard the flaws but shine a spotlight on the potential to improve or correct them. An unbiased opportunity to learn and change allows children to grow.

When you coach your child or students to move away from negative thinking, use examples that are relevant to them. If you know your child struggles with chores, bring that into the equation.

Instead of saying, "I cannot make my bed," encourage your child to say out loud, "I need to learn how to make my bed." This sets them into action. They now have some direction to ask a trusted adult to teach them to complete the chore well. Negative thoughts can often stifle creativity and behavior, but positivity can get people moving in the direction they need to go!

Role Models

Positive role models strengthen the fresh and open quality of a child's environment. Kids observe the impact of the role model's behavior and strive to incorporate that behavior into their own routines. You can introduce them to a diverse range of famous people who embody positivity in their daily lives.

- **Nick Vujicic:** An outspoken entrepreneur and orator, Vujicic was born with no limbs. With determination and boatloads of optimism, he is now a motivational speaker encouraging people to look on the bright side of the situation and simply try their best regardless of the odds.
- **Malala Yousafzai:** An incredibly courageous and strong activist, Malala promotes education for all, especially impoverished girls who struggle with inaccessibility. She survived a grave gunshot wound as a teenager and is now

renowned for her international commitment to freedom from oppression.
- **Bob Ross:** An avid painter, Ross used to host a TV show in the 1990s called *The Joy of Painting*. The episodes were notable for Ross's calm and joyful demeanor. He not only simplified the act of painting incredible pieces but covered various painting techniques and offered solace in the form of entertainment for an entire half-hour every week.
- **Oprah Winfrey:** Known for her rags-to-riches story, Oprah is famous for her generous personality and powerful persona on the screen. Often, she would give away funds and gifts to those in need and publicize the event to encourage people to find happiness in helping each other.
- **Fred Rogers:** A beacon of joy and aspiration, Rogers was a television personality who rose to fame for his consistent views on how kindness and goodness help a generation of children rather than any kind of negative reinforcement. He has written several books on growth and acceptance for children and adults.

Strategy 7: Encourage Group Activities

Be it for recreation, exercise, nonprofit, or career, any sort of group activity offers opportunities to cultivate substantial team-building skills and individual fortitude. Children gain a better hold on the various features of life and how different people are affected in their own ways. This skill can never be taught in classrooms and must be observed or experienced in person.

Sports

Popularly known as "for the jocks," the sports category invites those healthy enough to physically participate and learn. It challenges players of all ages with notable benefits. They

- Strengthen physical health.
- Boost brain activity.
- Contribute to teamwork.
- Embrace good sportsmanship.
- Form strong friendships.

Theater

Dramatic acting and dancing allow for bold expressions of emotion directed in healthy channels. Joining the drama club or theater practice helps.

- Improve creativity.
- Foster verbal and nonverbal communication.
- Encourage empathy and confidence.
- Strengthen body coordination.
- Cultivate strong partnerships and peer relations.

Debate Team

Joining competitive speech groups and debate teams caters to a child's perspective of the world and helps them build informed opinions on multiple relevant topics. Kids learn and practice in peer settings, thus familiarizing themselves with high-pressure situations while having to understand the importance of healthy arguments. The benefits help them

- Improve critical thinking.
- Enrich verbal communication and body language.
- Enhance patience and respect.
- Foster leadership skills.
- Boost confidence and self-esteem.

School Newspaper or Magazine

Various posts, including reporters, editors, cartoonists, and photographers, will be available on your child's school newspaper or magazine teams. Children will have the facilities to research additional information about current world events and be up to date with news about the school, students, staff, and the globe. They can

- Develop communication and language skills.
- Improve writing and editing.
- Interview people of varying expertise.
- Strengthen time management and deadline submission skills.
- Learn through experience.

Volunteer Groups

Participating in local or school volunteer groups helps students develop a better work ethic in general. They are able to appreciate the life they have while gaining the strength to reach out and help those in need. Volunteering allows kids to

- Foster compassion with no expectation of reward.
- Manage manual labor and simple paperwork.
- Learn secondhand about strife.
- Build resilience and confidence.
- Gain a better perspective on social awareness.

Strategy 8: Teach Conflict Resolution

Children experience a series of challenges throughout their formative years. These hurdles veer from mild to plain distressing. Such issues can have long-lasting negative impacts on a child's mental, emotional, and social well-being. Conflict resolution covers problems that arise from jealousy and bullying.

Handling Jealousy

Jealousy is an innate emotion that manifests in children as they develop their social and emotional skills. You'll see the most visible signs of this when they feel inadequate or abandoned or need attention and validation. Children can express different behavioral patterns, such as sulking, angry outbursts, or withdrawal from social interactions. Know that we simply can't avoid this kind of negativity all the time. Thus, it's important to create a safe environment where your kid feels comfortable expressing their feelings of jealousy so they can learn how to maneuver through it.

- Talk about insecurities. Share stories of when you felt insecure in the shadow of a more successful or fortunate person. Let your child learn that jealousy isn't an alien breach of normalcy but a part of everyday life. This way, they can exercise some control over reacting

adversely to the situation, knowing that this kind of thing affects everyone.
- Avoid comparing skills. This is an important rule relevant to many fields of research and not just parenting! When we avoid comparing skills, traits, successes, and even trauma, we allow kids to grow and heal at their own pace. For example, if we point out how Rebecca finishes her tests more slowly than everyone else in the class, we will give her a complex. She will feel shame at being the slowest test taker, and this will reduce her self-esteem. Instead, we must step up and help her practice formulating thoughts and writing more quickly to get her up to speed.
- Model behaviors and not feelings. It's ideal to focus on steering your child's actions and words rather than their emotions. We can't help what we feel, but we can practice expressing those emotions in healthier ways. When your child is jealous of their friend's or classmate's scores, you can suggest various options for them to try (study earlier, practice different problems, join study groups, or ask the teacher for additional help) instead of just telling them to not feel bad about it.

Managing Bullying

Bullying, both physical and verbal, poses a significant challenge to children and their social interactions. These acts range from name-calling and exclusion to physical aggression. Children who experience bullying are often the ones that suffer from low self-esteem, anxiety, and depression. We can advise kids to handle bullying in various ways, including avoidance, retaliation, or seeking support from trusted adults. Encourage open communication and foster resilience in your child. This will help mitigate the adverse effects of bullying on their overall well-being.

- We can't always avoid conflict. Bullies can target kids for no reason other than the latter were just in the wrong place at the wrong time. Sometimes conflicts cannot be resolved peacefully because the situation is controlled by the bully. We must be able to equip our kids to be able to think fast and flee successfully if necessary.
- Take deep breaths when stressed out. Teach your kid this form of controlled breathing when the adrenaline starts pumping. This will allow them to keep a mostly clear head when approached in an uncouth fashion.

- If you see something, say something. This is a crucial statement that applies to threats of many different kinds. But introducing young kids to this idea in a situation of bullying and conflict resolution helps ease them into it. Bullies look to gain control of an area by subjugating other kids. If enough children stand up to them, the instigator will retreat and ideally not bother them thereafter. If your kid sees another child being pushed around, embolden them to rally a small crowd of friends or other kids. It's an outstanding sign of support and power to stand up to an aggressor.
- Encourage your child to ask for help. Show them there is no shame in reaching out for assistance. You can demonstrate this by asking your partner, a friend, or your children to help with a chore or any simple task. This affects them deeply, knowing that they need not face the world on their own but accept social help or even community aid if the need arises.
- Reporting cyberbullying is a brave act. As children spend more time online, they will become vulnerable to online harassment, intimidation, and humiliation. Cyberbullying can take place through various online platforms, including social media, chat rooms,

and online gaming. Due to its anonymous nature, this form of conflict ranges from mildly challenging to even deadly in terrible cases. Victims of cyberbullying feel helpless, depressed, and socially isolated. Educate your child about responsible internet use, promote compassion, and help them develop coping mechanisms.

Strategy 9: Guide Them in Making Friends

Parents and educators will see a distinct difference in the ways kids form friendly connections as they grow. Preteens prefer independent thinking. While they're close to their trusted adults, they'll deliberately seek out peers from their neighborhood and school to gain the gratification of self-identity in a way grown-ups cannot offer.

Importance of Preteen Friendships

Pre-adolescent friendship explores the complexities of peer relationships even before children hit puberty and their teens. It is a fascinating landscape of emotions and growth, fluctuating constantly in the light of new people and new environments.

Children find a strong sense of belonging when they form bonds with close friends. It becomes a safe space for them, allowing them to improve their self-esteem, share experiences, play games, and spend time together.

These circles also encourage strong bonds that can lead to romantic attraction between children. Beyond just "hanging out," children formulate their identities and ideas by listening to their friends within the approved social circles.

Building Friendship Skills

These details from a *Raising Children* article (2021) show the influence of one healthy relationship on another:

Good parent–child relationships tend to lead to children having positive relationships with peers. So being warm and supportive, staying connected, and actively listening to your child can help them develop friendship skills. You'll also be better able to support your child if friendship problems come up. (para. 5)

It goes on to show the impact on children as they *recognize* the healthy traits of any relationship. When you spend time with your kid and affirm their confidence and choices, they will seek out similar flourishing connections with peers, choosing to move away from potential red flags. Friendships work on a two-way street, as the following points suggest:

- Compassion and gratitude must be reciprocated.
- Hanging out with close peers ought to elicit positive moods.
- Spend a suitable amount of time (not too little, not too much) with friends.
- Communicate well and avoid misunderstandings.
- Take care to not exclude a friend from gatherings. If this is done by accident, apologize sincerely and ensure it doesn't happen again.

A healthy social life is the result of a thriving upbringing. I don't mean your child *must* be a social butterfly. Even having a couple of close friends, in the long run, is far better than having a hundred fleeting acquaintances. The goal is to have a happy and well-adjusted kid!

Difficulties Making Friends

Many socially awkward children face trouble making friends. Kids of varying cultures are raised in contrasting environments and have different temperaments. If you've moved cross-country or traveled from a different nation, your kid will face small or large cultural barriers. Some may be able to overcome them with a little effort, and others need more time.

It can be difficult to allow your kid the space they need to foray on their own, but there are a few things you can do:

- Help them read social cues. This involves nonverbal communication and body language. When kids take the lead in conversations, they'll find their comfort zone with the right people.
- Let them try tasks on their own. Some independence is a fresh addition to their routine. Allow kids to buy something from a nearby grocery store or walk the dog on their own. Let them raise a plant or clean up their room as they see fit (after doing some research on their own). This improves their judgment as they develop their own choices. It helps them make better decisions when it comes to social connections.
- Encourage them to invite potential friends home for a snack or playtime. In this way, your kid can form bonds using the comfort of their home turf. Playdates and study sessions work well if they take place consistently over time.
- Take them out for group activities as an adult chaperone. Sports centers, clubs, a day at the park, or watching a movie or a game are great

examples of children having fun while socializing.

Balancing Friendships and Parent Relationships

Managing previous relationships while making new ones can be hard if your child is new to them. Children tend to hang out more with friends than at home starting from this age. As long as you know they're safe, this behavior can be encouraged up to a limit. Make sure to let them know that they can explore these multiple peer bonds while keeping you in the loop (even though that's not always guaranteed):

- Model healthy behaviors of balancing multiple relationships. Make it a point to keep in touch with extended family and friends once in a while. Your child will grow up seeing you put in that constant effort.
- Make time to connect with family. Set up simple game nights so no one relies on screens and instead spends time with the family.
- Encourage your child's socialization with their new friends. Praise your kid's decisions when they make good choices and guide them when they make mistakes.
- Be cheerful to your kid's friends as well, but not overly so. Preteens are learning independence

and opt out of adult supervision. Allow them their space. This also lets them know you're "chill" and are approachable when they recognize trouble.

Strategy 10: Discuss Nonverbal Communication

By this age, most kids are aware of communication beyond spoken or written language. Tonal changes, body language, and facial expressions contribute a lot to a conversation. Children start using sarcasm and hyperbole as they watch you do so. Some kids do not pick up on these cues for a variety of reasons ranging from lack of exposure to an inability to comprehend such behavior.

Sign Language Benefits

Light practice encourages kids to observe your body movements and facial changes that contribute to what you say. One of the best examples of this is sign language. Aside from outright communication, sign languages incorporate the advantages of nonverbal communication.

You can consider any form of sign language, such as American Sign Language and its dialect Black American Sign Language. These show how speakers don't just express words with hand poses or signals but also change their facial expressions and body language. They move just about every aspect of their body to express the emotion behind any explanation.

Learning sign language will engage your child in strong body momentum and teach them how expressive every movement can be. It's a wonderful lesson to learn, and those fluent in it can convey a variety of sentiments and opinions without making a single sound.

Demonstrate Nonverbal Cues

Here are some examples of nonverbal cues that you can demonstrate to your child. Use the given actions to emote clearly:

- **Confident:** Sit up straight or stand tall with your feet slightly apart, make brief eye contact with the people in the room, relax your shoulders, and look calm and poised.
- **Nervous:** Bounce your leg if you're sitting or tap your foot if you're standing, frown at the ground, sigh once in a while, and fiddle with your hair or clothes.
- **Afraid:** Sit or stand stiffly, hunch your shoulders, gulp once in a while, widen your eyes, avoid eye contact deliberately, and, if possible, try to perspire or hold back tears.

- **Impressed:** Lean forward to stare at or listen to the person you're impressed with, raise your eyebrows in delight, and look excited but calm enough to stay quiet.

Avoid Misreading Body Language and Cues

- Practice demonstrating emotions using specific body poses and facial expressions. Kids can learn to exaggerate these poses at first and then try subtler styles.
- Try games and activities where one child embodies the cues to show how they're feeling, and the others guess the exact sentiment. Guide them to use body language maneuvers while speaking passionately about a favorable topic.
- Set up a short play where children can use their theater skills to dramatize their speeches and conversations using cues. Let them pick their approach to this. Correct them during their practice run so that when they demonstrate in front of a group, each kid plays their role correctly.

With some practice and confidence, kids can use body, face, and voice cues in daily conversations!

Strategy 11: Teach Patience

This article from *Greater Good Magazine* talks about Pamela Cole's research on how children struggle with patience (Calechman, 2019):

The main question of "Why is waiting so hard for kids?" has a few more fundamental answers. One is that their lives have been about you being there for them, and—with a seemingly benign phone call, a book that you began reading, or a conversation between parents—you're suddenly not. "It's not a threat, but it's unsettling," Cole says. "It's not conscious, but they're always motivated to maintain the connection." (para. 8)

You can help ease this break in connection by allowing your child or students the time to gain a different kind of engagement simply by waiting.

Practice Patience

Self-reflection is a great way to have children consider their own approach to being patient. This second look at the situation from a meta-perspective can sometimes help remove the urgency of the issue or offer other ways to reduce the stress of it. By "perspective," I mean the child's point of view, which always seems so solid to them.

You'll notice 11- and 12-year-olds have a much better understanding of self-reflection, so you can lead them to the jumping-off point and watch them leap forth! Let them explore how the situation changes when they change perspective. Let them consider your busy schedule from your point of view. Why is it important for Mom to get ready for work early every day? Why should Dad be busy with lunch before noon? Kids will understand that it takes time to be ready for the following tasks. Preparation precedes work, and this is a lesson that takes a bit of time to fully sink in. But once your child realizes it, they can appreciate the work.

Patience is also better guided by positive affirmations. Coach your child to motivate themselves so that when you aren't immediately available, they aren't floundering right away. Encourage them to embrace small distractions if it helps them while away the time waiting.

Kids crave some kind of intriguing stimulation, and it can feel borderline exhausting to always be on the move! Even if they are unable to stay calm all the time, remind them that they've tried their best and it's okay to need help staying patient. Perfection isn't the goal, but working on the process always helps.

Delayed Gratification

Working with the understanding that instant gratification is to be avoided, you can focus on delaying rewards and approvals. Allow your kid to understand the benefits of exercising self-control, first by gifting them small rewards when they show restraint toward something, and second by providing appropriate praise.

For instance, your child's bike is sent to the repair store to address a brake issue, which will take a week. Now your kid's job is to figure out how to plan their week, not by moping around for the bike, but by keeping themselves calm and occupied.

- Use distractions. Show your kid that they can divert their attention for a while by focusing on other entertainment. Your child can spend time discovering long-lost games the family hasn't played in a while!
- Try something new. Introduce your kid to a new hobby or an interest. This can be academic or leisurely, but as long as the kid is able to learn something of value, it's a two-for-one deal! They can build an old-fashioned lemonade stand, start a collection of funky pebbles and coins, or find and press beautiful flowers.

- Try something challenging. The time that would have been spent riding the bike can be used to try their hand at a difficult task. Or you can even teach them to collect coins and dollar bills to save money. Coach them on how to save a small amount from their weekly allowance. Praise them for the consistent amount they keep aside if they manage to keep this up beyond the first week.

At the end of the week, congratulate their patience in being able to wait for the bike while managing other things.

Strategy 12: Teach Respect

People With Disabilities

It's important to promote inclusivity and compassion toward individuals with different physical, sensory, and cognitive disabilities.

The words you use to describe their experiences must be regular. Use "matter-of-fact" language to explain the reality around people who live with chronic conditions. This involves explaining their treatment or adaptive equipment, such as cochlear implants, crutches, wheelchairs, and portable oxygen tanks.

Take care to provide accurate information about disabilities while negating myths and taking stock of stereotypes. If you do not find the right TV shows or movies that portray certain impairments correctly, take the time to research online and find people with lived experiences of special needs.

Encourage Curiosity While Respecting Others

You can point out certain similarities between your child and the person in question in a gentle manner to try and bring some aspect of relation. But that's not always possible, so it's best to allow your kid to ask you the tough questions rather than being abrasive to people with disabilities.

Sometimes, you may come across people struggling with rolling their wheelchairs up a slippery ramp or someone with a cane waiting to cross a busy road. Guide your child to politely ask them if they need help before trying to assist them. And remember—if they say they're fine, there's no need to bulldoze over their words! People with disabilities who've lived with their diverse experiences absolutely know what they're talking about.

Understanding Consent

Practicing consent is a vital life skill to introduce to young children. It's important to demystify consent, ensuring that kids understand the significance of personal boundaries and respect for others' choices. Education on consent is relevant to all relationships, whether personal or professional.

Implement role-playing exercises so your kid can practice asking for and giving consent. This will help them develop the confidence necessary to establish boundaries and respect the autonomy of others, thus reducing instances of ungainful teasing, bullying, and harassment.

Child 1: "Do you want to play tag?"

Child 2: "No, I have to finish my homework."

Child 1 now has two options. They can respect the second child's answer or try and drag them out into the playground. Ask the kids which option is appropriate and why.

Sometimes, children receive a "no" without a reason. This ought to not change their respect for the person, depending on the severity of the situation.

Inspiring Role Models

Discuss role models that may inspire your child to be the best person that they can be. Role Models may be anyone in all of history. We are all a part of the human family. Although modern-day thinking may push your child towards being an individual, make sure they understand that being an individual does not mean being selfish or self-centered. The most remembered and beloved role models were those who strove their whole lives to help humanity in peaceful, loving ways. If force were ever used, it was only to defend the weak, innocent, and sacred.

In every corner of our world, in every generation of time, there were people who stood up for others or did things to improve the world for the whole family of mankind. Your child may have heard of some of these inspiring people in school, church, or perhaps in their own neighborhood. Someone who was honest, trustworthy, or who, through a series of small acts, achieved something amazing.

Here are examples of some people in history who accomplished amazing things:

- **Jesus Christ:** He was the son of a Jewish Carpenter named Joseph. Many throughout the ages believe he is the literal son of God. Though he was hated by the Jewish Leadership of his time, he taught people principles through parables and his actions that have had a positive influence on the whole world. He taught about love and duty, avoiding hypocrisy, and even how to stand up to those who bully others. He forgave people and taught people to change their lives by changing the way they live. His words are still quoted in our day, and they are some of the most wonderful and beautiful words ever spoken.

- **Michelangelo:** An artist who created incredible statues out of stone with just a hammer and chisel. He developed a talent he had and worked at it, sometimes making the same statue over and over until it was perfect. In 1508, Pope Julius II commissioned him to paint the Sistine Chapel. One brush stroke at a time, he created inspiring images that resonate with love and dedication to this day.
- **Mohandas Karamchand (Mahatma) Gandhi:** An Indian Lawyer during the time that Great Britain had control of India, who witnessed the great inequality and atrocities that the British committed on his people and led his people through the philosophy of non-violence to seek independence from Great Britain which he achieved in 1947. Gandhi's approach to non-violence inspired others to take up the cause of Civil Rights and use non-violence all throughout the world.

- **Martin Luther King Jr.:** In the United States, Martin Luther King Jr., in the 1960s, led American Black people on peaceful marches, which angered White racists into committing violence against them. This shocked the country and changed laws to make the lives of Black people better. Other groups have used similar methods to improve their civil rights since that time.

Though these people are well-known, your child can find role models that make a difference every day through their jobs. Nurses use their knowledge of medicine and patient care to treat patients with respect and kindness. Scientists try to improve our knowledge of the world. Teachers have been known to sacrifice much to help children learn. All people, regardless of the circumstances, can do wonderful things for others.

Disabled people can also accomplish wonderful things! Ludwig Von Beethoven became deaf and still created great music. Anne Sullivan, a partially blind teacher, taught blind and deaf Helen Keller to communicate, learn numbers, and read braille, and Helen went on to write and take on Political ambitions that were radical for her day.

Strategy 13: Set Expectations

The ability to understand how rules help us navigate our environments will contribute to your child's maturity. Start with the simplicity of household rules. Explain the reason behind the most common ones.

- "Why do we keep our elbows off the table during meals? It's so nobody's arms are pushed off the table in case there's less space between plates."
- "Why do we avoid screen time just before heading to bed at night? This helps us relax our eyes in time to feel properly sleepy and also gives our devices a long break."

Children may question your rules from time to time out of curiosity and annoyance. If your explanation doesn't seem valid or if they're able to poke holes in the "logic," consider having a lengthier, more meaningful conversation.

Safety Comes First!

It's necessary to know the rules of your location. If you take your kids to the public pool, ask them to search for the safety rules posted in the area. It's often a board with a numbered list printed near the entrance or somewhere else in plain view of everyone. When your child spots it, take the time to go over the rules. If everyone follows these regulations and stays safe, you can all have fun in the water!

Morals Go Beyond Fables

Rules of morality are more than the respectful manners we are all expected to follow. They are also about the kindness we show to our fellow humans. You can model this behavior of compassion in a public place. Return a cart from the parking lot to the supermarket or throw litter in a trash can. Your child will follow suit and be good without throwing fits every time you ask them to be ethical.

Let them know that even in a difficult world, others will appreciate kind actions when they choose to be moral and courteous to people and the environment.

Health and Hygiene

You can do your best only if you're healthy enough. Often when kids get "troublesome," it's because they may be overstimulated or feel "off." Encourage them to be mindful of their own health. Follow general and daily hygiene expectations such as morning ablutions, showers or baths, and regular handwashing.

A well-balanced diet with less fast food and processed meats allows for a healthy lifestyle. If this is followed by the whole family, even the youngest kids will be more willing to acquiesce.

Real World: Advanced Mode

To prepare your kids for the greater difficulties of the outside world, share your experience with them in whatever manner possible. The more relevant your memories are to their situation, the better. For instance, share a story of when you reached an event late and disappointed people. Focus the story on how you sincerely apologized for the tardiness and thanked others for being somewhat patient.

There is no need to brownnose anyone. Simply convey the sentiment of your remorse and authenticity: "The real world may wait for you to fall, but you need to encourage yourself and get back up. Remember, I believe in you, and I love you! Are you proud of yourself?"

KIDS' CORNER!

You're about that age when you understand that the world is way bigger and people are so much more complex than you initially thought. Discover what you're interested in. Curiosity can be a gift when you know exactly how to approach other kids and grown-ups to learn more than what your school gives you!

There are a few ways to find out what there is to know about your ideas.

1. Talk to People

Who?

Check out the place to find your targets. Maybe there are some kids your age who know what they're doing. They'll probably be your best informants.

Find the grown-ups you trust. They will be in uniform or will have a badge to signify they work at the location. You'll get closer to your answers if they know the topic you're curious about.

How?

Be polite. Other kids can be super shy or wonder if you know more than them! By asking them questions gently, they'll know that you're simply curious and would love to help you out. But if they don't answer right away, don't push them. Give them their space and see if you can find an adult.

Ask them to spare you some time because most adults are always busy! They're figuring out how to balance their day, and you can help by approaching them like you would tip-toe toward a kitten.

Alright, I was kidding. But it's still better to just be nice to them, not because that's how you get your answers, but because your goodness can be the best quality about you.

What?

It helps to articulate exactly what you're looking for. Practice communicating well using your words, tone, body language, and facial expressions. Ask good questions to get good answers. If you're worried about asking a stupid question, is it because your parent or teacher may make fun of you? That's not fair! If it helps, ask a friend, and be cautious so they understand that this is important to you. A real friend might laugh, but they'll also help you.

2. Use the Internet Well

Where?

If asking humans leads you nowhere, find the sacred interwebs. I'm sure you know what to do online, but here's a quick crash course.

Search engines are a gem. Google is the most popular one, but you can access more data by using different search engines such as Brave, Firefox, DuckDuckGo, and Ecosia. Each one has its pros and cons about privacy, security, and free access to articles.

Be careful about your security. You can check with your family or teachers on internet safety, but there is incredible information online that can teach you just as well. For the best results, read up on these with a trusted adult so they can learn alongside you.

3. Crack Open a Book

When?

At what point do you think an offline resource works better than online stuff? Possibly when the answers you're looking for are old or if the internet doesn't give you all the details. Libraries with literal books are the best treasures scattered around the world. If you're lucky, you can find notes from people who've checked out that book before you!

Why Are We Talking About Learning?

When we learn about the world, we understand more about ourselves. This includes the exact way we should go about learning.

Curiosity helps build the features you want to grow up with. The way you use this in life explains a bit about yourself. Reaching out to people around you is sometimes the best way to learn about them and the place you're in. It helps to ask them directly rather than going behind their backs.

Communication

Use verbal and nonverbal communication. Yes, you can absolutely send secret messages without using words! Sign languages are an excellent way to talk without talking. When you show strong or soft emotion using your face or body movements, you're letting people know how you feel about something. You can even practice this with your friends and develop your own secret language without words.

Empathy and Respect

It's also important to respectfully agree or disagree with people. The main part is that you stay friendly with your besties even when you disagree! Listen to them when they argue, ask careful questions to understand their point of view, and wait your turn before explaining your side of the problem.

This also helps you understand the difference between a forceful "no" and an enthusiastic "yes." Consent is important to give and receive. If you make a mistake, take the time to go back and learn more about the situation. Apologize to people if they are hurt and work on the answer. Your friends will also help out if you're empathetic and try your best.

Patience

When possible, share your good fortune and help others when they ask for it. This is the same in reverse: When you need help, don't be afraid to ask for it from family or friends.

Everyone we meet has a complex and full life with trials and tribulations, highs and lows. It pays well when we wait and allow people to explain their side of things. We never know the journey another human is going through. So, let's not simply downplay someone else's experiences.

We're near the end! Remember, stay true to yourself. Be kind, explore, and have fun.

YOUR CHANCE TO HELP EVEN MORE KIDS

Your child is leveling up, and to give them the best chance possible, we want to level up their peers too. This is your chance to help!

Simply by sharing your honest opinion of this book and a little about your own experience as a parent, you'll show new readers where they can access the Social Superstar Strategies.

YOUR OPINION MATTERS!
LEAVE A REVIEW TO HELP OTHERS JUST LIKE YOU

Thank you so much for your support. Together, we can help a whole generation.

CONCLUSION

There is no perfect parenting handbook or educational guide because every child is different. As soon as you figure out how to manage a healthy relationship with one kid, along comes another who throws you off your game!

As a parent or guardian, you are your child's first teacher. Your baby imprints on you and perceives you as their entire world. Your kids grow up with your values and ideas. Raised well, they will be able to branch away from your sphere of influence and cultivate their own identity. This shouldn't come as a shock to you. It is a bittersweet moment to watch your children figure things out without your guidance, but the truth is, they are constantly relying on your past teaching moments.

Every decision they make, and every action they take is reminiscent of your influence on them. Every conversation you've ever had with them resonates with their choices.

Social Skills for Kids (Ages 5 to 12) helps you empower an entire generation of children who are just beginning to acquaint themselves with the outside world. I know the feeling when you are at your wit's end because your kids seem to struggle way more than you can ever help them!

CONCLUSION | 239

Confident interaction does not come naturally to everyone. That's why I've offered you the Social Superstar Strategies that were such a hit with my children! They're quite grown-up now and are well-adjusted individuals with healthy relationships across the board. Believe me when I say I learned far more than I expected throughout their childhood. The nuggets of knowledge throughout this book are from my experience and the lessons I've picked up along the way.

I invite you to put these strategies into action and foster the seeds of empathy, respect, and cooperation in your child. Let's prepare them for a world that values not just beauty and intelligence but also the warmth of understanding, kindness, and shared humanity.

Children are more than our future leaders and innovators of society. They are also individual people determined to carve out a path for themselves through the world. As educators and guardians, it's our duty to impress upon them the virtues of respect, compassion, and acceptance.

We've covered the guardian's role when it comes to nurturing social skills. Life is dramatic, and it's three times more intense backstage, and that's where you're working! Modeling the cohesive skills of sharing, cooperation, and listening sets the groundwork for a lifetime of solid and wholehearted personality. We want our kids to grow up strong yet kind; genuine but not gullible; open to helping, and ready to receive assistance as well. These are not contradictions but rather show the duality possible when we make an effort to let our children learn from our actions and the world's responses rather than just flat words.

The goal is to raise a self-sufficient child who can take on challenges, learn from failure, stay resilient through tough times, and know when to ask for help.

You may never know all the facets of your child but do your best to let them understand that they don't need to hide their fears from you. And definitely don't shame them for hiding certain truths! There are many factors in the world that influence them. If you do a great job equipping your kid with the tools they need in their formative years, they'll grow up to be strong, independent, kind, and respectful—not just to the world but to themselves as well.

ACKNOWLEDGMENTS

This book would not have been possible without the guidance of Rasmus and Christian Mikkelsen, Karina Sanchez, Brian Chang, Ed Fahy, Rob Cerecedes, and Rebecca Pierce, who taught me how to put a book together right.

Help with writing and editing came from K.C. Alvida and Clara Dunne.

Christopher Dexter was responsible for getting Midjourney.com to produce AI images for the interior.

PublishingServices.com handled the Formatting.

The book cover was designed by Sherwin Soy.

Finally, a special thanks to CSD Digital Enterprises, LLC, who put this book out into the world.

Josh Evermore

REFERENCES

Anderson College. (2015, May 6). *Tips for resolving conflict when working with preschoolers.* https://www.andersoncollege.com/tips-resolving-conflict-working-preschoolers/

Auletta, K. (2022, June 22). *14 kids tv shows that celebrate diversity.* HuffPost. www.huffpost.com/entry/kids-tv-shows-celebrate-diversity_l_600ade92c5b6a0d83a1aa8f9

Bamford-Beattie, C. (2022, April 5). *How can I prevent cyberbullying?* Kidslox. https://kidslox.com/how-to/prevent-cyber-bullying/

Bandura, A. (1977). *Social learning theory.* Prentice-Hall.

Bayless, K. (2022, May 26). *How to help your child make friends.* Parents. https://www.parents.com/kids/development/friends/making-friends/

Be Strong International. (2021, March 16). *How to teach children the value of following rules.* https://bestrongintl.org/programs/how-to-teach-children-the-value-of-following-rules

Bologna, C. (2019, August 20). *35 children's books that teach empathy and kindness.* HuffPost. https://www.huffpost.com/entry/childrens-books-empathy-kindness_l_5d52e7b1e4b0c63bcbee2699

BSA Admin. (2015, March 10) *10 children's books that teach diversity.* Bright Start Academy. https://www.brightstartoverland.com/10-childrens-books-teach-diversity-2/

Calechman, S. (2019, June 11). How to teach siblings to resolve their own arguments. *Greater Good Magazine.* https://greatergood.berkeley.edu/article/item/how_to_teach_siblings_to_resolve_their_own_arguments

Catholic Early EdCare (2021, March 03). *Why developing social skills is important for young children.* https://www.catholicearlyedcare.qld.edu.au/why-developing-social-skills-is-important-for-young-children/

Centers for Disease Control and Prevention. (2023, June 6) *Important milestones: Your child by five years.* https://www.cdc.gov/ncbddd/actearly/milestones/milestones-5yr.html

Common Sense Media. (n.d.-a.). *Best international films for kids.* https://www.commonsensemedia.org/lists/best-international-films-for-kids

Common Sense Media. (n.d.-b.). *Movies that inspire empathy.* https://www.commonsensemedia.org/lists/movies-that-inspire-empathy

Common Sense Media. (n.d.-c.). *School movie night picks for K–5.* https://www.commonsensemedia.org/lists/school-movie-night-picks-for-k-5

de Saint-Exupéry, A. (1943). *The Little Prince.* Reynal & Hitchcock.

Dr. Seuss. (1990). *Oh, the Places You'll Go!* Random House.

Elder, B. (2020, January 15). *Puppet play: How to help your child self-regulate their emotions and behaviors.* Integrated Learning Strategies. https://ilslearningcorner.com/2020-01-puppet-play-how-to-help-your-child-self-regulate-their-emotions-and-behavior

Faber, A. & Mazlish, E. (2002, September 01). *How to talk so kids will listen... and listen so kids will talk.* Simon & Schuster Audio/Nightingale-Conant.

Gowmon, V. (n.d.). *Inspiring Quotes on Child Learning and Development.* Healing for a New World. https://www.vincegowmon.com/inspiring-quotes-on-child-learning-and-development/

Haller, S. (2020, November 24). These 8 toys crush bigotry and stereotypes. Yay for raising inclusive humans! *USA Today.* https://www.usatoday.com/story/life/parenting/2019/11/15/toys-kids-crush-stereotypes-and-teach-diversity-barbie-dolls-lego/2574415001/

I Am Expat. (2021, August 23). *The benefits of group activities for children in childcare.* https://www.iamexpat.nl/education/education-news/benefits-group-activities-children-childcare

Kamenetzky, K. (2022, May 18). *How to help your elementary schooler make friends.* Verywell Family. https://www.verywellfamily.com/here-s-how-to-help-an-elementary-schooler-make-friends-5199194

Kazdin, A. & Rotella, C. (2009, January 27). I spy daddy giving someone the finger. *Slate*. https://slate.com/human-interest/2009/01/your-kids-will-imitate-you-use-it-as-a-force-for-good.html

Kennedy-Moore, E. & Lowenthal, M. S. (2011). *Smart Parenting for Smart Kids*. Jossey-Bass.

Kluger, J. (2020). This disability rights activist wants to be the first wheelchair user in space. *Time*. https://time.com/collection/davos-2020/5764739/eddie-ndopu-space/

Krajewski, S. (2020, July 20). *100 children's books about diversity and inclusion*. The Art of Education University. https://theartofeducation.edu/2020/07/july-100-childrens-books-about-diversity-and-inclusion/

The Manthan School. (2023, April 12). *Patience is key to success: Teaching students about patience and self-belief*. https://www.themanthanschool.co.in/blog/patience-is-key-to-success-teaching-students-about-patience-and-self-belief/

Mischel, W. (2014). *The marshmallow test: Mastering self-control*. Little, Brown and Co.

MVP Kids. (2022, June 3). *Supporting positive outcomes using puppet play*. https://www.mvpkids.com/activities/puppet-play-at-home-ages-and-stages

Naître et Grandir. (2021, September). *7–8 years old: Social development*. https://naitreetgrandir.com/en/step/5-8-years/development/7-8-years/fiche.aspx?doc=child-7-8-years-social-development

Nolte, D.L. (1998, Jan 1). *Children learn what they live*. Workman Publishing Company.

Ortiz, C. (2020). *9 disabled activists from the queer rights movement*. Disability Pride Week 2020. https://sites.duke.edu/disabilitypride2020/artwork/queer-rights/

O'Shea, K. (2012, May 7). *10 secrets of helping your child make and keep friends*. Parent 4 Success. https://www.parent4success.com/2012/05/07/10-secrets-of-helping-your-child-make-and-keep-friends/

Raising Children. (2021, September 13). *Friends and friendships: Pre-teens and teenagers*. https://raisingchildren.net.au/pre-teens/behaviour/peers-friends-trends/teen-friendships

Reed, P. (Director). (2015). *Ant-Man* [Film]. Marvel Studios, Walt Disney Studios.

Made in the USA
Columbia, SC
12 June 2025